inmost being. Further

MEDITATION, ECSTASY, AND ILLUMINATION
An Overview of Vedanta

MEDITATION
ECSTASY
AND
ILLUMINATION

An Overview of Vedanta

Swami Ashokananda

Advaita Ashrama
(Publication Department)
5 Dehi Entally Road
Calcutta 700 014

Published by
Swami Mumukshananda
President, Advaita Ashrama
Mayavati, Pithoragarh, Himalayas

Distributed by
Vedanta Press
1946 Vedanta Pl. - Hollywood CA 90068
e-mail: info@vedanta.org

First Edition, March 1990
First Impression, July 1993
5M3C

Printed by
Gipidi Box Co.
3B Chatu Babu Lane
Calcutta 700 014

PUBLISHER'S NOTE

PUBLISHER'S NOTE

Swami Ashokananda joined the Ramakrishna
Order in 1921 and took the vow of Sannyasa in 1923
from Swami Shivananda, second President of the
Order. He served as the editor of the *Prabuddha
Bharata*, English monthly organ of the Ramakrishna
Order, from 1926 to 1930 and was Swami-in-charge
of the Vedanta Society of Northern California, San
Francisco (founded by Swami Vivekananda in 1900)
from 1932 till his passing away in December 1969 at
the age of 76.

The Swami rendered great service to the cause of
Vedanta movement in the West by his clear and
thorough expositions of Vedantic teachings through
lectures and classes for nearly four decades. During
his ministry the Vedanta Society expanded its
activities greatly, adding to it two sub-centres and two
forest retreats and a new temple at San Francisco.

From 1953 onward the Swami's lectures were
recorded on tape. The present group of eight lectures
was selected to give the reader an overall view of
Vedanta with its historical background as well as with

its theoretical and practical aspects.

We are thankful to the Vedanta Society of Northern California for editing these lectures and making them available to us for publication. We hope that this selection will serve as an introduction to future collections of Swami Ashokananda's lectures and classes and will be of benefit to those who are aspiring toward the goal of spiritual life, whatever their chosen path may be.

Advaita Ashrama
Mayavati
1 March 1990

CONTENTS

CONTENTS

THE TEACHER-PROPHETS OF
VEDANTA

1

Those of you who are acquainted with the principles of Vedanta must have recognized that they are universal and eternal in character. Even if Vedanta is thought of as a religion — which it is, in addition to being a philosophical system — one finds that it does not exist on anyone's authority; it is impersonal. In India we have always taken the attitude that truth is its own justification and foundation. It does not require the authority or support of a person; rather, a person, to be worthwhile, requires the support of truth.

So from ancient times in India efforts have been made to find truths — truths which are ordinarily called 'supernatural', but which are as impersonal as the laws of external nature — and it is claimed that at least four thousand years before Christ a great body of such truth was discovered. In spiritual knowledge, the highest truth is utter unity, and it is probable that this highest truth of all was discovered earliest. Such a

statement no doubt appears strange, because, after
all, the highest is always the culmination of a
process; it is not reached first. However, so far as
we have records, we find that the discovery of the
unity of everything, the utter unity of the individual
and the universal, beyond which nothing can be
conceived, is recorded in one of the earliest hymns of
the *Rg-Veda*. I have sometimes mentioned this to you
with gladness, because the person who is considered
to have arrived at this truth was a young woman, the
daughter of a Vedic sage. Her name was Vak. Some
say that this account must be allegorical, because *Vāk*
means speech, or the goddess of speech or of wisdom,
and probably the name Vak was just a reference to that
goddess. But there is no reason to think that, because
afterwards there were others who arrived at the same
truth and were celebrated in the ancient books. This
young woman, then, was the first to realize that there
is only one Being and that she was herself that Being.
She composed a beautiful hymn, which is even now
sung whenever the ultimate Deity is worshipped as
goddess. So the very highest truth was arrived at in
those earliest recorded times. Of course there are
many preceding stages of spiritual realization, all of
which were described in later Vedantic texts; in fact,
it can be said that the three main stages of spiritual
experience are represented in the Vedanta.

I think I should explain very briefly the word
vedānta. You know, the body of religious literature
called the Vedas is the most ancient in the world. A

good part of the Vedas was lost at an early time; it is conceded that probably the major part is forever gone. But whatever remained became systematized into four books by a very great sage, named Veda Vyāsa. (Vyāsa was his original name, but because he worked on the Vedas, the word *veda* became permanently prefixed to it — Veda Vyāsa.) He divided the Vedas into four books: *Ṛg-Veda, Sāma-Veda, Yajur-Veda,* and *Atharva-Veda.* Each Veda, again, is classified into different sections. There is first of all the *Saṁhitā* portion, which is composed of hymns, usually written in verse. Then comes the *Brāhmaṇa* portion, usually written in prose. At the end of the *Brāhmaṇas* there are sometimes philosophical discourses, which are called *Upaniṣads* or *Vedanta.* Each Veda has also been differently divided; for instance, sometimes the ritualistic portion is called *Karma-kāṇḍa,* and the philosophical portion, *Jñāna-kāṇḍa.* Or sometimes they have been divided into the *Saṁhitās,* or hymnal portions, and ten *Āraṇyakas,* or forest books, which are more or less composed of the *Brāhmaṇas* and the *Upaniṣads.*

Now, here we are concerned, of course, with the very last part of Vedantic literature, which is called Vedanta — *veda anta,* 'the end of the Vedas'. Many have thought that these portions came last of all in the Vedic age: at first the ancient Aryans practised rituals; then afterwards, being dissatisfied with rituals, they began to become philosophical and to find philosophical truths, which they embodied in the books generally called the Upanishads, or, in aggregate, the Vedanta. Others have said that this chronological explanation is not right. What *anta* really means is 'the highest' or 'the culmination'. *Veda* means 'knowledge'; therefore *vedanta* means 'the end of knowledge', 'the highest knowledge'. Orthodox Hindus believe that the second explanation is more appropriate, because the philosophy contained in the Vedanta portion is also found in the hymnal portion. For example, some hymns in the *Ṛg-Veda* and the *Atharva-Veda* cannot be surpassed in their philosophical and mystical depths even by the Upanishads. Of course, Western scholars have said such hymns were afterwards interpolated. Well, orthodox Hindus do not agree with that. They say that from very ancient times both the ritualistic portions and the philosophical portions existed simultaneously.

You have to admit there is justification for that belief, because in actual spiritual life both ritual and philosophy have validity, if not for the same person, at least in the life of the community. A large number of people have to depend upon ritualistic or similar practices in order to arrive at a condition where their spiritual life can be entirely contemplative. Why should it not also have been so in those ancient days? Well, however that may be, there certainly was a period, lasting probably two thousand years, when philosophical speculation was much more emphasized than at any previous time and during which a great deal of energy was given to the search for and finding of hidden spiritual truths.

The Upanishads, in which those truths were expressed, are sometimes called 'secret teachings', and no doubt the word *upaniṣad* has some such implication – not secret in the sense of mysterious, but in the sense that these truths are not found on the surface by the average mind; they are buried deep down and have to be discovered by everyone in his inmost being. Further, when these teachings were given to a pupil, the pupil approached the teacher and sat near him, and the teacher gave this teaching to him alone, not in the presence of others. Even now, these teachings are given in private. Others are not allowed to be present, because it is considered that anything given out publicly can never take root in the deep life of a person. Just as the roots of a plant generally die when they are exposed to the sun or the outside atmosphere, in the same way whenever you express something it fails to go deep into your life, and you hate therefore to speak in public of the deepest things; they should be kept hidden within. On this psychological fact the tradition of privacy was built.

Now, as I said, it probably took two thousand years to develop and consolidate these teachings; that is the orthodox Hindu belief. Many would not agree with it, but when I consider how long it takes to find one single truth, and when I remember that the truths expressed in the Upanishads were not inherited by these people but had to be *discovered* by them — when I consider these facts, I cannot but think that the orthodox Hindu belief is correct.

As I said, the principles of Vedanta are universal. What are these principles about? Because they are concerned with ultimate reality, they are about anything you would call real — the world, for instance. And certainly, I, for myself, am real, and I want to know the last word about myself; so the soul or the Self is discussed. And since there was a belief in an ultimate Being, there was a great deal of speculation about God. In other words, Vedanta considers the same problems that every other philosophical system considers — God, soul, and the world. Along with that, many other things are involved. For example, Vedantists have given a great deal of thought and time to the discussion of different states of mind or of consciousness, which they found very important for the determination of truth. Other topics were also discussed, some that have no real significance for us today, and some that can help us a great deal. Of course, much has probably been lost, but enough is left.

It is said that there are altogether a hundred and eight Upanishads. It is quite obvious that most of these are not true Upanishads at all; that is to say, they did not form a part of the original Vedas but were written afterwards. From that you should not conclude that they are worthless; as a matter of fact, some are highly illuminating and explain many things not found in the original Upanishads, which some scholars have said number twenty-eight. Of these twenty-eight, some say twelve and others say ten are the principal ones. Shankaracharya, to whom we owe the revival of Vedanta after Buddhism degenerated, commented upon ten Upanishads, and therefore many think that these ten must have been the most authoritative. Two of them — the *Chāndogya* and the *Bṛhadāraṇyaka* are very large and in many places very abstruse. In fact, one is compelled to confess that some passages cannot today be explained at all. Other Upanishads are smaller; some are composed of just a few verses. But all of them have been considered of exceeding value, and as century has followed century very great authority has been ascribed to them.

Some Upanishads are written in verse, and others in prose and some are mixed prose and verse. The language, which is the Vedic rather than the classical style of Sanskrit, is sometimes obscure, but more often it is very straight and direct. As you read the texts you feel an atmosphere of sunlight, of open spaces, of the frankness, the innocence, and the purity of childhood. You feel that the people who dwelt upon these thoughts and experiences and gave expression to them were sturdy men, strong men, but not violent. (Violent people are weak; truly strong people are gentle, pure, and innocent, and their gentleness is not associated with any kind of weakness.) You also feel that there was not much restriction in their life. By that I do not mean there was licence, but that there was no rigidity about them, and you feel that you would rather like to go back to those people; you cannot escape the feeling that they represented the highest expression of life on earth; that they were highly civilized and highly cultured.

The life they lived, these people who taught the Upanishads, was a very simple life, mostly. But sometimes these teachings were originally given by kings who lived in the luxury of a palace. There is a theory, which Swami Vivekananda himself held to some extent, that the Vedanta, or the Upanishads, really originated among the *kṣatriyas*, the warrior caste, rather than among the *brāhmins*. And in support of this we often find in the history of India that the most liberalizing thoughts in religion or philosophy came not from the first caste, not from the *brāhmins*, but from the second caste, the *kṣatriyas*. For example, Sri Krishna was not a *brāhmin*; he was the son of a *kṣatriya*, and Buddha, who democratized the teachings of the Vedanta and spread them broadcast, was the son of a *kṣatriya* king. We do not consider this to be a reflection on the *brāhmins*; we say that just as two opposite forces create a balance, so in every community or every system of knowledge there have to be two forces working — one conservative and the other liberal. If liberalism has complete freedom in its own experimentation, it is apt to kill itself; therefore, there has to be a conservative force that will challenge it. When liberalism can stand that challenge it is gradually embodied into the accepted authority. In India the *brāhmins* have represented that conservative force, and in the matter of Vedanta we find that some of the teachers were *brāhmins*, others were *kṣatriyas*. So we sometimes find *brāhmins* going to *kṣatriyas* to learn this most excellent truth, the truth about the Atman and Brahman.

Well, whatever that might be, most of these teachers lived a simple life in an *aśrama*, which can be translated as 'retreat'. Just as modern retreats are located outside the cities in a solitary place in the midst of nature, so in those olden days there were many such retreats or hermitages all over the country, particularly in the Himalayan region. And many of these teachers — who were generally called *ṛṣis*, which literally means 'seers', because they directly perceived supernatural truths — were established in these *aśramas* and were supported by the rich or by kings, who considered it their duty to protect them and to supply their needs.

Those needs were very simple. They lived in huts; they would get up at what they called the *brahma-muhūrta*, the 'hour of God', an hour before dawn, and would go in the dark or semidark to a nearby stream and bathe; then they would sit around a fire, which was always burning, but which at that time was burning brighter because the disciples had put more logs on it, and they would plunge into meditation. After long meditation some teachings would be given, and then they would all go to their respective duties. Later, classes would be held in the different branches of learning, particularly in the Vedas and the Upanishads; the *ṛsis* would teach their pupils the art of meditation; they would teach them what is called *brahma-vidyā* — the 'science of Brahman', or the 'science of God-realization', and they would teach them philosophy, so that their intellect would be trained in accordance with their spiritual findings. There were also other teachings, sometimes called *vedāṅgas*, which were essentially secular subjects like astronomy, prosody, grammar, and so on. The pupils themselves had to live a life of utmost asceticism, of which the most essential condition was the practice of celibacy. Many rules are given in the old books for this rigorous life. The pupils would live many years with the teachers, whose examples were considered very important as a part of their training. Then some of them would return to the world, get married, and live as ideal citizens. They would not give up their spiritual practices; rather, they would carry them on, and when they were fifty years old they were supposed to retire from the world and plunge again into a life of contemplation and meditation. And then, after some time, they would embrace the life of utter renunciation and become *sannyasins*, or wandering monks. That was the general picture.

It goes without saying that although there might have been hundreds and hundreds of such hermitages, not all the *ṛsis* were equally proficient. It is but natural that there were differences among them, and you find that some became very well known as great spiritual teachers and as great scholars of the Vedas or Vedanta. Of course, more people would come to them than to others, and one to whom thousands and thousands of people would flock used to be called *kula-pati*, the 'chief of the clan', the clan of spiritual aspirants. Such 'chiefs' were very highly regarded, and necessarily used to receive great respect from all. And of course the kings and the nobles of a kingdom considered it their special duty to support them.

You can understand why the people amongst whom Vedanta originated lived in a very quiet place where their meditation would not be disrupted or interrupted, where there would not be even the slightest noise, for only in that silence, external and internal, were they able to discover inner truths unknown before. They practised hard austerities; you can see why that had to be so: how would they know there were deeper states of mind to begin with? Only the other day in the West you began to talk about the subconscious mind and to recognize that there are many things hidden in the mind which have great meaning for our conscious life. You see, even the science of the mind seems to be a modern thing with us. So in order to find ultimate truths, these *ṛsis* had to work very hard. No doubt many of them came up with wrong knowledge. They thought they had found something extraordinary, but the mind is a very subtle and complicated thing. When you think you have found something new and begin to talk about it, others find that it was not new or anyhow not valid. So while there must have been many experimenters who found something true, there were also many who became deluded. You can well see that it must have taken centuries and centuries before enough authoritative knowledge was gleaned, out of which a system of mysticism and a system of philosophy took birth.

2

I said at the outset that the principles of Vedanta are impersonal. Of course, all principles are impersonal, but it is also true that if spiritual principles are not embodied in a life, they are as good as nonexistent. How shall I know that there is such a thing as God if He has not become real in my own life? The deeper the principle the greater the necessity that it become alive and real for us. The action of material forces is obvious to us; even if we do not know how lightning comes or what makes the crash of thunder, the effect is there. But even the effects of spiritual principles seem unknown to us; at least, we do not recognize them as such. How much more difficult it must be to discover those principles themselves! So you see, although we may not look upon a person as the authority behind the principle, still the necessity of a person in whom subtle spiritual truths have become real, is paramount. We cannot have any religion or any true philosophy unless we have its exemplars amongst us. So we have given a great deal of respect to these ṛṣis.

If you ask an orthodox Hindu what the authority is for his belief, he will first of all mention the Vedas. Well, of course, everyone will cite his own holy book as an authority: an orthodox Christian will say the Bible is the authority; a Mohammedan will say the Koran is the authority; so when a Hindu cites the Vedas as the authority, it doesn't seem to mean anything more than that. But if you press our Hindu further, he will say the ṛṣis are the authority. In other words, he would say that there have been generations and generations of people who have made these truths real in their own lives, who have actually experienced them; *they* are the authority. If you press him still further, he will say, 'Well, I would not swear by them. I have to experience those things myself before I know that they are really true'. I think in this respect the Hindus are a little unique. They say that we ourselves have to experience these truths; there is no use just believing in them and thinking that some Saviour will come and rescue us whether we experience them or not. No. They will admit this much: great saints and sages, particularly those who are called Saviours – we call them Incarnations of God – have the power of making you experience these truths. Nevertheless, whether it is by our own direct effort or through the grace of an illumined soul, *we* have to experience these truths ourselves, *here*.

Otherwise, we do not think we have arrived at any certainty of knowledge. About that, every Hindu is quite decided; none would say, 'The books have said such and such, and if we do this or that, then we shall go to heaven, and there's the end of it'. Or 'We shall take the name of the Saviour and he will take care of the rest'. No. We have never accepted any such belief.

About two things we have been very decided. One is the place of ritual in spiritual life.[1] Long ago the Hindus came to the conclusion that rituals have value but won't take you to the highest. In advanced spiritual life it is not ritual but knowledge or devotion that is important. Devotion is also a kind of knowledge; it is state of mind; it is not dancing or singing or repeating something. Such activities may bring about a favourable inner condition, but in the direct perception of spiritual truth action can have no place; it belongs to the lower phase of our being — our body and our superficial mind. About this the Hindus are very sure.

They are also very sure that spiritual truth has to be experienced here. Faith or belief or the assurance that we may realize it after death — none of these things have any place in the Hindu's mind. You realize truth here, then you have it. If you don't realize it, you don't have it. Of course the Hindus believe that if you

---

[1.] *See* 'Ritualism: Its Place in Spiritual Life' in this volume.

have not realized spiritual truth in this life you will come back; you will be given any number of opportunities. You will be born a thousand and one times if you want. But think of the trouble of coming here again and again, again and again in order to learn something! We want to finish soon and get rid of the necessity of being born.

So those teachers who have the power of making us experience spiritual truths have been highly regarded in India, and we have high regard also for those who have embodied these truths in their lives. We recognize that even a great philosophy might become just a dry shell devoid of substance if great souls were not born to keep it alive. Religions die that way, philosophical systems die that way. You have in the West wonderful idealistic systems, by following which one could become a great saint. For instance, I believe if anyone followed Kant's system, he would become a very great mystic. But you see, nobody ever thinks about following it. They think about reading it, arguing about it, interpreting it, or finding fault with it. All of which is nothing but a labour of the intellect. Intellect is not the Spirit; intellect is part of the mind, which is very different from the Spirit.

Every system has to be made alive by living examples of its truths. In every generation in India there have been such exemplars of Vedanta, and each of them could be looked upon as a prophet, although I myself would not go so far. In determining who the prophets of Vedanta are, I would say first of all that the *ṛṣis* who discovered the essential principles of Vedanta would naturally be called the first prophets of Vedanta. In discovering those truths they embodied them. *Brahma veda brahmaiva bhavati*[2] – 'He who knows Brahman becomes Brahman.' Next, those who later discovered the same principles in their own lives, and felt the urge to spread them amongst others could be called prophets, or teacher-prophets. You see, this urge to spread the teachings of Vedanta requires a little reinterpretation of the original teachings. Thus Sri Krishna of the *Bhagavad-Gītā* can be called a prophet of Vedanta; Shankara is another, and I would also include Buddha. Then there is a third group: those who might not reinterpret Vedanta in any sense but who have, as it were, put greater strength into an earlier interpretation and teaching, so that in their own age they were a tremendous force for the reactivation of these spiritual principles. There are these three groups.

In this lecture I will speak only of the first and second groups, and I have already spoken about the first group in some detail. I think its members were legion, and although we know only a very few of their names, we do know some. It is an odd thing that the Hindus, who are supposed to have no historical sense, are very keen about spiritual genealogy, and so in the

---

2·*Muṇḍaka Upaniṣad,* 3. 2. 9.

Upanishads you sometimes find long lists of names. Such and such a *ṛṣi* learned this truth from so-and-so, who learnt from so-and-so. Back and back it goes, and when you come to the beginning, you find the Creator. The first teacher was the Creator, God Himself. There is a very interesting theory that God could not create this universe unless at the same time He created the Vedas. You must admit that if you want to do something, a plan for it must be in your mind. In other words, there is simultaneously a mental scheme and a concrete creation. The whole universe, with all its laws, all its interrelations, is contained in the mind of the Creator, and then this concrete universe flows out of His mind. So it is said that the Vedas were created at the same time that the creation of the universe took place. Therefore in the first stages of the creation there were some persons to whom the Creator gave these Vedas, and then, generation by generation, they came down to the days of the Upanishadic *ṛṣis*. Well, these genealogists prove at least that the knowledge of Brahman, the Vedanta, was treasured by them: they took great care to protect it, and they revered their original teachers.

It was recognized that there could be two or three different opinions on a certain topic. But afterwards all these views were synthesized, and there came into existence a book called *Brahma Sūtras* or *Śārīraka Sūtras* or *Vedanta Darśana*. These three names are given to it. *Brahma Sūtras* – aphorisms regarding Brahman; *Śārīraka Sūtras* – aphorisms regarding the embodied. Who is embodied? The Atman is embodied. I am embodied; that is to say, I have a body; I am the Spirit and I have a body. God also has a body; this concrete universe is His body. So they say that these aphorisms pertain both to the Self and to Brahman or God. And *Vedanta Darśana* literally means the philosophy of Vedanta. This book of aphorisms was divided into sixteen parts: each four of which made up one chapter. Its author is also called Veda Vyāsa, as was the man who systematized the Vedas.

Now, of the first group of the prophets of Vedanta only their names are known; we don't know any particulars about them. Sometimes no name is given; only anonymous teachings are placed before us, and we have to contemplate upon them and realize them. The teacher was always supposed to be a knower of these truths. It is laid down in several Upanishads, and it was a general practice: *tad vijñānārtham sa gurum evābhigacchet samitpāṇiḥ śrotriyam brahmaniṣṭham*:[3] 'In order to attain the knowledge of Brahman, one should approach a guru with firewood in hand', *samitpāṇiḥ*, that is to say, fuel in hand. What kind of guru? He should be *śrotriyam*, 'well versed in the śruti'— in the Vedas and the Vedanta — and *brahmaniṣṭham*, 'well established in Brahman'. Some have said Brahman here means Vedas and others have said, 'No, Brahman here means God'; the verse means that the

---
[3.] Ibid., 1. 2. 12.

teacher must not only have philosophical knowledge but *also* spiritual knowledge. So although we do not know the names of all these prophets, we know that they had gigantic minds and were well established in the knowledge of Brahman.

We always think of that age as the most glorious in Indian history. Those extraordinary men and women, who brought their senses and minds under control, who did not crave anything of this world, whose faces were luminous with the light of Self-realization, of God-realization, and who embodied this truth in their being — those men and women moved amongst the people. Many of them were wanderers; they would sometimes live in their *āśramas*, but at other times they would roam over the country with their disciples. Of course, it was very wonderful to have them come to the cities or the villages. I must admit that it sometimes must have been inconvenient, too, because, after all, to entertain such large numbers of people was not easy for the householders. However, this is the picture that comes to our mind: We see our country dotted over by these wandering knowers of God, and the people to whom they came would receive their knowledge. It is still the tradition today for *sannyāsins* to wander around, and amongst these so-called wandering beggars you will find great philosophers and great knowers of spiritual truth.

Here I think one point is worth discussing: these ancient *ṛṣis* had a tendency to represent truth in as logical a way as they could. Of course, in the

Upanishads the arguments are not given in full; you could not expect that. When they were composed writing was not known, and so they had to be composed in very brief form to facilitate memorizing. But there was always the oral tradition, which afterwards became what we call *bhāsyas*, or commentaries. You really cannot understand the Upanishads unless you read their commentaries along with them. You will find that what is given in simple and brief form in the text is elaborated into long and complicated philosophical interpretations and arguments. Well, you know, when you read such things you have infinite possibilities for the exercise of your own intellect.

But only when you have undergone spiritual discipline or only when you have studied with one who has actually experienced these truths, would you know which interpretation is justifiable and which is not. Today in India if you say, 'I have studied Vedanta; I am well versed in Vedanta', they will ask, 'Who was your teacher? With whom did you study?' And if you say, 'I studied by myself', no good! Or if you say, 'I studied with such and such a person', 'Was he himself a knower of Brahman?' 'No, he was a great scholar.' 'That won't do.' If you say, 'Why not? He had a keen intellect'. 'That's not enough.' Intellect is a strange thing. It is like a lawyer's brain; it can take any thesis and make it relevant. That is where intellect falls into a trap. You might think whatever is logical is true. But how do you know that you have found what is logical?

Until you have found the error in your argument it seems logical. So there is always a doubt about it. Therefore it is said *tarka apratiṣṭha*, 'reason is without foundation'. You think you have found the foundation, somebody else finds a flaw in your argument; the bottom drops out. Intellect is always subject to this difficulty, but spiritual experience is not; so you have to study with someone who is himself an embodiment of spiritual truth. Well, during the many, many centuries in which these *ṛṣis* lived, they impregnated the country with the consciousness of the spiritual truths they had realized. And India has never been able to get away from them — cannot get away from them.

3

The prophets of the second group are, of course, historical, although there is a good deal of legend mixed in. Their lives are vivid to us, and they had this extraordinariness: most of them are considered to have been Incarnations of God. We do not know how or when the doctrine of Divine Incarnation arose in India, but certainly it arose before Christianity. It is now historically proved that Sri Krishna was worshipped as an Incarnation of God long before Christ was born. It is known that the *Bhagavad-Gītā* was composed before Buddha lived, and it is generally recognized — although there are some differences of opinion — that the religion represented in the *Bhagavad-Gītā*, the Bhagavata religion or devotional religion, arose at least at the time Buddha was born. It is known that it coexisted with Jainism and Buddhism. Some say that it arose much earlier, at the time of the Kurukshetra war, which is mentioned in the beginning of the *Gītā*. In any event, Indian historians are agreed that the Kurukshetra war took place about fifteen hundred years before Christ. We would not be wrong in saying, therefore, that Sri Krishna, the first of the second group, lived in the fifteenth century B.C.

He was an extraordinary person. Of course, many stories that are told about him cannot be historically proved, and many of the acts ascribed to him seem purely legendary, because they cannot be considered natural. Other things, however, he unquestionably did: First of all, he brought together all the teachings of Vedanta into a form that became very appealing to the people. You find this teaching embodied in the *Bhagavad-Gītā*, which he is supposed to have uttered on the battlefield of Kurukshetra to his friend and devotee, Arjuna. Whether Sri Krishna said all the things that are contained in that discourse is doubtful. It seems unnatural that at the very beginning of a battle he would have had an opportunity of giving such a long talk; the other party probably would not have permitted it; they would certainly have wondered what he was doing, giving a three-hour-long discourse. It is doubtful that the teaching was actually given at the time in such elaborate form. But considering his life as it is represented in the old books such as the *Mahābhārata*, the *Harivamsa*, and so on, it seems right to think that the *Bhagavad-Gītā* is representative of his teachings. The person who is said to have composed this book is, again, Veda Vyāsa, who is also supposed to have composed the *Mahābhārata*, of which the *Gītā* is a part. What do we find in the *Gītā*? It is said, *sarvopaniṣado gāvaḥ* [4]— 'All the Upanishads are, as it were, cows', and Sri Krishna is the milkman; the *Gītā* was the milk, and Arjuna was the calf. The idea is that the Gita represents the very essence of all the Upanishadic teachings. That is the general view, and I think it is more or less correct. But in the *Gītā* Sri Krishna gave a slightly different emphasis to these teachings; he stressed the *karma-kāṇḍa* or action portion of the Vedas, and so *karma yoga*, action as a path to God-realization, is an important part of the teachings of the *Gītā*.

Secondly, Sri Krishna introduced the teaching of Divine Incarnation. As I said, we do not know how that doctrine originated. In the days of the early Vedas there was an acceptance of the idea that when a person realizes God he becomes God. I mentioned to you a young woman who, having realized her identity with God, began to think that it was she who had become everything, the gods functioned at her command, the world was created and destroyed at her will; she began to feel herself to be the universal Being. There are other mentions of such experiences in those old books. Well, the doctrine of Divine Incarnation is similar to

---

[4]. *Bhagavad-Gītā*, 'Meditation', 4.

these ideas, except in the *Gītā* it is said that God Himself becomes born as a man, not that man, having attained to perfection, becomes God. These are two different ideas; certainly they have different emphasis, and both are current in India.

Sri Krishna was the first Incarnation of God properly so recognized. (Some say there was another before him, named Rama, the son of a king; yet I think Krishna was really earlier than Rama. And although Rama is worshipped by millions in India, particularly in northern India, as an Incarnation, he did not leave many teachings and we will not discuss him here.) Sri Krishna no doubt brought to the world a tremendous spiritual power, and if the stories are to be believed, he left a deep impression on his contemporaries all over India. But as I said, he is more or less a mythical figure and we haven't much historical information about him; therefore we cannot say how great his influence was in his own time. Yet it is true to say that his influence through the centuries — about thirty-five hundred years — has grown, not decreased. And in modern times he has become better known than ever, both in India and outside India, through the many translations of the *Bhagavad-Gītā*. Everybody wants to translate the *Gītā*, and of course those who read it cannot escape thinking about the personality of Sri Krishna and of his manifold activity. His way of being tremendously active while representing the highest ideal appeals particularly to the modern mind, because modern people are caught in the complexities of action and yet want to feel detached, free of these things, not dragged on by them; so we find the teaching and the example of Sri Krishna a great stimulus.

After Sri Krishna we come to Buddha, who lived about the sixth century B.C. Of course, Buddha is not thought of today as a Vedantist. But he himself felt he was part of the community of the Hindus and that he was teaching some of the essential things taught by Hindu saints. For centuries afterwards the Hindus did not think of the followers of Buddha as separate from themselves. You see, the idea of many religions, one separate from the other, is a modern and essentially a Semitic idea: you add 'ism' or 'ity', and you classify all people and put them in watertight compartments, and there you are. That which should be the basis of unity becomes the source of difference and separation. That idea is certainly the brainchild of Western man; it has nothing to do with the Orientals. A Chinese could be a Confucian and a Buddhist at the same time; he could also be a Christian. You would not know where he stops being a Christian and starts being a Confucian or a Taoist or a Buddhist. He gets mixed up there. In India there are Christians who worship in Hindu shrines and Mohammedans who worship at Hindu shrines, and Hindus who worship in Mohammedan shrines. It is very difficult to keep them separate; we have never tried to. And we have looked upon Buddha as a Vedantic prophet. As a matter of fact, in one of the old books he is sometimes called *Advaya-vādin*, the 'teacher of monism', teacher of

Advaita. And that he really was, only his approach was different.

He took the Vedantic teachings and spread them broadcast for the benefit of all. Previously only a handful of people could study the Vedas; Vedic Sanskrit itself took years to learn. So he gave the same teachings in the language of the people. And he used a simple approach; he said quiet the mind, get rid of things. Well, if you get rid of things, what remains is Brahman. Vedanta also says that. But since Buddha wanted to speak to the multitudes, who didn't have much learning or know much philosophy, he dispensed with all the complexities of philosophical argument; he simplified everything. If Sri Krishna extracted the essence of the Upanishads or Vedanta for the benefit of all, Buddha democratized the same teachings so that they could be given even to those who were not of Aryan culture, who had no philosophical knowledge, who didn't know Sanskrit, who were not even educated. You see, these moral teachings, the teachings of nonself, appeal to all. Of course, the teachings of contemplation are always difficult for people everywhere; not many are willing to sit down and meditate. But the rest of Vedanta he made very easy.

And not only did he present the teaching of Vedanta in a slightly different and popular form, but he was the first amongst all religious teachers to become a missionary. The word *missionary* has a bad odour about it, but take it in the right spirit. Buddha said to his monks, 'Go, go to the east, go to the north, go to the south, go to the west and spread this wonderful message of *nirvāna* or enlightenment to all'. He wanted his disciples to give everyone this good information. Just as amongst the early Christians the idea was to spread the Gospel, the good news that the Saviour had come, so amongst the early Buddhists, about six centuries before Christ, there was the same tendency. This, then, was the contribution of Buddha: His own personality was tremendous; he simplified the teachings of the Upanishads, and he made Vedanta a missionary religion for the first time, spreading it beyond the borders of India to all peoples. Even if you don't accept the idea that Buddha was really a Vedantist and that all he taught was Vedanta, the astonishing thing was that although his missionaries went in the name of Buddhism, very soon they began to teach all kinds of Indian philosophical systems, and today, because so much was lost when northern India was ravaged by foreign invasion, we can recover ancient Sanskrit texts, to which we have references but no manuscripts, from their translations in Tibetan and Chinese. You see, the Buddhist monks spread Vedanta everywhere they went.

Buddha also introduced organized monasticism in India. I would not use the word *organization* in connection with the ancient *ṛṣis*. It was left to Buddha to organize monasticism as an institution; he was the first person in the history of religion to establish monasteries and lay down rules of monastic living. It was one thing for a wandering monk to go from place to place; the rules by which he was governed were the rules of his inner life. But when you have one hundred monks living together, then other rules have to be instituted so that they can live together in peace and with profit. Buddha was the first to institute such principles of discipline. All these things he did.

After Buddha there came a long period during which there were many teachers, but none were of such prominence, and I won't go into details. Then we come to Shankaracharya. Shankara himself did not really contribute anything new to the teaching of Vedanta — not even a new emphasis as did Sri Krishna and Buddha; yet he figures very prominently in the history of Vedanta and is undoubtedly one of its greatest teacher-prophets. He was born in the south of India in the late eighth century. When he was just a boy he left home and wandered until he came to a teacher in central India of whom he had heard — a great *sannyāsin* and knower of God, whose name was Govindapada. The story is that he was waiting for this disciple, but probably that was an afterthought. In any case, when this boy came Govindapada was highly pleased and taught him everything that he knew, and under his instruction Shankara realized Brahman; that is to say, he attained to the highest knowledge. And then the teacher blessed him and before he passed away told him that he must reestablish Vedanta.

What did he mean by 'reestablish Vedanta?' As I have said, there were the Upanishads — a hundred and eight or twenty-eight or twelve or ten, as you may consider it — which were the original texts of Vedanta philosophy and religion; then there was the *Brahma Sūtras* or *Vedānta Darśana* and there was the *Bhagavad-Gītā*, which contains the essence of the Upanishads. These three bodies of scripture are called the main sources of Vedanta, and Govindapada wanted Shankara to establish them on grounds that could not be assailed by anyone. You see, in those days there were great Buddhist and Jaina philosophers and strong leaders of other religions. The country had become, as it were, divided into many warring sects. In actual practice, there was not much religion left, but there was a lot of intellectual talk. The ancient knowledge of the Veda and Vedanta was lost, and it was left to Shankara to reestablish it. And that is what he did. He composed most extraordinary commentaries on ten main Upanishads, which are still unsurpassed by anyone. Even his opponents have not been able to find fault with any of his writings or with the way he has supported Vedantic views. There has not yet been a single error discovered in his arguments, which shows what a clear intellect he had.

Then he wrote a voluminous commentary on the *Vedānta Darśana*, and also a commentary on the *Bhagavad-Gītā*, which is considered to be the oldest of all its commentaries and which is still the crown of the many commentaries written since. In addition, he wrote many independent texts, some of which are very well known, and composed many hymns and poems.

That is only his writing side.

He had many disciples, whom he trained in the Vedanta philosophy as well as in *Ātma-vidyā*, realization of the Self — actual direct perception of the Self, mystical realization. He established many monasteries all over India. His four main monasteries in the four corners of India — north, south, east, and west — are still in existence. He reestablished the old Vedantic monastic order, dividing it into ten sections, which themselves are also still in existence.

He went from one end of India to the other, meeting the founders and the leaders of all kinds of sectarian religions, meeting Buddhist and Jain philosophers, defeating every single one of them in argument, and converting them to his views — the condition of debate always being that whoever was defeated must accept the philosophical views of his opponent. And then, having accomplished all those things, he passed away in his thirty-second year.

He was a most extraordinary person. Of course, his greatness lay in his not wanting to give a contemporary emphasis to the ancient teachings of Vedanta; rather, he wanted to present them as they had been presented in ancient times. Some maintain that he was such a monist that when he came across texts which clearly indicate dualistic or qualified nondualistic views he could not do justice to them. Others say no, he gave the right place to everything. Well, let us grant that he may have been a little enthusiastic about his monistic views and may have done some injustice to texts which really indicated other views—even so, we have to admit that his interpretation remains unassailed. The dualistic realization, the qualified monistic realization, and the monistic realization are all clearly stated in the Upanishads, and when Shankara says they represent different experiences but that the ultimate experience is the Absolute, I think he does justice to the ancient teachers.

So Shankara, truly speaking, revived Vedantic culture in India, and, as Swami Vivekananda once said, that process of reformation or revival is still going on; Shankara's work has not yet reached its culmination.

4

The last prophet of Vedanta I will speak about is Sri Ramakrishna, who lived in the last century; he was born in 1836. Now, Sri Ramakrishna had a unique desire to practise all religions, to follow all the paths as given in the texts and as prescribed by the great teachers, and to come to the ultimate realization by way of each of these paths. It took him about ten to twelve years to accomplish this, and out of his experiences he came to certain conclusions. He found that all these paths—all the different sectarian teachings of Hinduism, the teachings of Christianity, and of Mohammedanism—all these bring a person to the direct experience of God. He found, also, that in this realization of God there are indeed different stages. In the first realization, which is dualistic, the soul does not feel its unity with God, and yet it perceives God, just as the subject of a king can stand before the throne and see the king but cannot believe that he himself is like one of the royal family. He then found that when the soul becomes more intimate with God, that is to say, when communion becomes deeper and the soul loses a little more of the earthliness which had kept it separate from God, it begins to feel a basic unity between itself and God, though distinction still remains. Afterwards he found that the soul becomes completely lost in God, becomes one with Him, and of that realization nothing can be said. He used to illustrate it by saying that if a salt doll goes to measure the depths of the sea, before it has proceeded even a few steps it melts into the water — who, then, would measure the sea? From his own experiences he found these different views of God not contradictory. Dualism is not a contradiction of monism but is only an earlier step. You start with a dualistic realization of God; then you realize the qualified monistic state, which was taught by Ramanuja;[5] then afterwards you come to monism; that is to say, you become one with God. This is what Sri Ramakrishna found. He also found that all religions follow certain basic principles: all of them teach that earthliness must go from the soul; all of them teach self-discipline; all of them teach longing for and devotion to God; all of them teach that God is Spirit,

---

5. *See* 'God and God-Men in Vedanta' in this volume

not matter, that God is eternal, not temporal; all of them teach concentration of mind and at-onement with God. He found that what has been taught in Vedanta has really been taught by all religions; wherever people have found any truth, they have found the same truth. And so by his own experience he proved that there is a harmony among all religions that exist.

Further, he found that in these warring times, when ideas are clashing with ideas, religions fighting religions, people fighting people, Vedanta can stand for the basis of universal harmony. In Vedanta there already exists a philosophical and religious system which does not say to others, 'Oh, you are wrong; you must be converted'. He said, 'Look here, we have always known that all these paths and beliefs are true. Why are you fighting us? And why should we fight you?' So his chief disciple, Swami Vivekananda, came to the West and spread broadcast the fact that if you study Vedanta you will find the essential explanation of all religions, both in theory and in practice.

Swami Vivekananda taught what Sri Ramakrishna had proved by his own life. And because they were both men of profound spirituality, this teaching is not merely an expression of thought conceived by a clear intellect. I am sorry to say that whatever power ideas may have, they are not powerful enough in themselves to bring about changes in human life. People do not always understand that; they think if an idea is good it will have influence. As I said earlier, ideas may influence our intellect, but as we all know, our life is often very different from our intellect. To change our life so that it will accept what our intellect understands requires another kind of power, and that is spiritual power.   Unless words and ideas have this power behind them, they will not be able to influence human minds. Unless ideas come from people who have actually realized them, made them real in their own lives, they haven't much value in the life of mankind. That is why prophets, in the sense I have been using the word, are necessary.

I am very glad that we have a prophet for these modern times — a prophet who says every path is good, every path that the human soul is walking is good; there is a basic unity in everything. In spite of all errors and mistakes, all souls are going towards God, towards that highest goal. Furthermore, the basic principles of Vedanta need to be reiterated at this time, reiterated again and again, because these are the things we need to remember now. If you study the life and teachings of Sri Ramakrishna and Swami Vivekananda, you will find that a flood of light will illuminate all the dark patches of our existence and make what is so complex simple and what is so dark clear.

THE THEORY AND PRACTICE OF MONISM

1

As you all know, monism is a philosophical and
religious theory which holds that the ultimate reality
is one. There are, of course, several theories or isms in
regard to the nature of ultimate reality. For instance,
in addition to monism there is dualism, the view that
there are two realities – the soul and God – and that
they are separate from one another. Truly speaking,
dualism is a sort of pluralism, because it not only
maintains that the soul and God are two separate
entities, it also holds that there are innumerable souls,
and that there is, of course, an insentient reality
called the world. So although the term *pluralism* is
used for philosophies that explicitly maintain that
there are many realities, every dualistic theory is
actually pluralistic.

Then there is an ism in between monism and
dualism that is called qualified monism. Philos-
ophically speaking, qualified monism can be said to be

allied with monism, but in spirit, it is dualistic. All qualified monists, you will find, are devotees of God; they maintain that the souls are distinct and different from God. Distinct in the sense that while they are not the same as God, they are not independent realities completely cut off from Him, and different in the sense that God is *vibhu*, vast, and the soul even in its perfect state is *anu*, atomic. That is to say, the souls are distinct in nature from God, although they, as well as the world — which according to qualified monists is insentient — are all held together in one reality, all subsumed in the being of God — not separate and outside of Him. Just as our concept of a tree contains branches and leaves and flowers and whatever else there might be, all distinct from one another, and certainly distinct from what we call a tree (we cannot call a branch or a twig or a leaf a tree), similarly, the qualified monist's concept of God contains within itself the distinct presence of an infinite number of souls and the insentient world — all are bound up together, not separate. Therefore, the view is called monism, but since it is not pure monism it is called qualified monism.

What I want to discuss this evening, of course, is monism. I think most of you have a general idea of what is indicated by the term *monism*. In our present experience, we are aware of several kinds of reality. There is first of all the soul or conscious entity. Then there is the mind, and there is the body. We know that our body is made up of living matter, and we are also aware of dead matter, of which this universe, to our present understanding, seems to be formed. In short, we see an infinite number of conscious entities, we find many living forms, and we see this vast world of dead matter. All these things seem to be somehow governed by laws, which we are trying to discover through the study of science. And of course, either because of inherited superstition or tradition or whatever it might be, we cannot altogether forget the existence of God. You might say that God is not a matter of experience to us now; nevertheless, God is certainly one of the dominating ideas in our mind. So all these things you could call realities. Now, according to monism, the differences and distinctions that we now make between the living and the nonliving, the conscious and the unconscious, between one soul and another, between the soul and the world, between the soul and God, and so on — all those distinctions are our mistakes.

That we are prone to make mistakes must be admitted; we are full of ignorance. Many of the authors of books on Vedanta, particularly monistic Vedanta, point out that in explaining the state of things and in trying to find the truth we should take into account the presence of a pervasive ignorance. If I have some disease of the eye, then certainly I must take this fact into consideration in deciding whether or not things are really as they appear to me. If a person were suffering from jaundice and found everything yellow, he would certainly take this fact into consideration.

He would say, 'Probably the yellow does not belong to things; it might belong to my eyes.' He goes to a doctor and has his jaundice treated, and after he is cured, he finds some things white,   some grey, and so on; then he is sure he is seeing rightly. Vedantic authors give this kind of illustration and warn us that we must not ignore the fact that our knowledge, our motives, our feelings, our instincts are all somehow flawed by a mysterious ignorance. They say if you trace everything to its source, you will be surprised to find that this world is not at all various; there are not many kinds of realities here; all these distinctions and differences are due to our ignorance. If this ignorance were not there, we would not feel that we have these garbs of mind and body in which we are enclosed, and, therefore, we would not feel that we are separate from other beings or from God. They come to the conclusion that since ignorance is not to be considered as something actually existent, actually real, there is only one reality. Vedantic monism starts with that idea: there is just one reality, one *Being*, one infinite, eternal Consciousness; according to the monists, that is the ultimate reality, or the only reality that exists.

Some of you will raise the question that if the ultimate reality is a conscious entity, then how do you account for unconscious entities. The answer that is given is that they are only appearances. Suppose twenty people tried to represent a sitting room. Some would take the posture of chairs; others would stand as lamps; others would take the garb of a table or a desk, and some of course would be human beings seated in the chairs. Everything in that room would really be a conscious entity; only the *forms* would differ. Some forms would appear as forms of dead things, as of a chair, others would appear as forms of living things, as of a man or a woman, but all would really be living beings. They say that everything in this universe, whether it be the most conscious human being, like a Christ or a Buddha, or the deadest of all things you could think of, like a grain of dust or a particle of stone — everything differs only in form; behind these dead or living forms is the conscious entity. If you ask, 'Would not that consciousness find expression?' no, if it chooses to remain hidden, if it wants to become a chair — well, it will try not to appear as a moving or breathing chair. (From that idea has come the corollary idea that it is God who has, as a sort of game, taken all these infinite forms, living and nonliving.) Monists say that a person can actually reach a state of apprehension in which he will see this living God, this conscious Being, even in a dead thing, that is to say, even in material things. In other words, this conclusion of monistic Vedanta is proved by one's own experience. If it were not proved, it would be a most drastic speculation and of little good to us.

One thing we cannot ignore: If a thing is not established in truth, it will not last. Because our relative existence is not established in truth, it is perishable; every moment it is changing, and through these momentary changes it is coming to that grand change called death — decay and death. If you say that if it exists for a moment there must be at least a momentary foundation to it, yes, there is a momentary foundation. But it so happens that we are not concerned with, nor are we satisfied by, momentary existence. Some philosophers might tell you that you should be satisfied with one day's existence or fifty years' existence; why bother about permanence? But you must admit that your whole process of mind, whole motive for action, whole scheme of life is based on the idea that things are permanent. From one point of view you might say, 'No, we don't want things to be permanent; that would be a horrible prospect'. From another point of view, if things were not permanent you could not breathe for the next moment and could not plan for any day. Just consider that everything is momentary, perishable; let it enter into your mind. To put it crudely, suppose you knew that everyone were going to die tomorrow — would you be able to live today? So I say, although we do recognize the perishableness of things, at the same time we assume that everything is permanent. And why do you think we make that assumption? Because we really *are* permanent; there really *is* a Being that is eternal.

I am trying to tell you that there is a quest within us for eternal truth or reality. You cannot explain it away; nor can you ignore it. All philosophy, all religion, all stable forms of existence, all recognition of ideals and pursuit of ideals even through strife and struggle, all those things presuppose that there is something eternal and permanent. If there were not, everything would become meaningless; all philosophizing and religious pursuit would be absolutely inane.

Modern people have taken this attitude: 'Let me live my present life well; the next life will take care of itself.' No. You would not know how to live your present life well unless you had taken into consideration your whole life. You have to know what you are reaching for. Then in relation to that goal you determine every part of the process by which you reach it. What you do today should be determined by the ultimate goal of your existence. Fortunately, we have that feeling of permanence; we can never forget it.

Let me tell you a story from the *Mahābhārata*. There was a great king who was considered to be the embodiment of the highest virtues. It is said that the God of Righteousness one day wanted to test him; so he took the form of a stork — what a form to take! — and he stood on the shore of a big lake. Now, this king and his four brothers were wandering in the forest, and they were very thirsty. The king said to his youngest brother, 'Go and see if you can find water.' The youngest brother found a wonderful lake — and there was this stork. He said, 'Stop, prince!' You see, in those days birds and beasts and trees and gods and human beings all spoke the same language and understood one another. We have become too crass now. Well, the stork said, 'You must answer my questions, and if you cannot answer rightly I won't permit you to drink this water. If you violate my

words and drink this water, you will at once die.'
The prince was very thirsty; he thought, 'What is
this nonsense from a bird!' He drank a little water,
and he fell down dead. Of course, he did not return
with the water. So the next youngest brother was sent,
and he also did the same thing. The four brothers came
to the lake, drank a little water, and died. The eldest
brother, the king, waited and waited. Hours passed,
brothers didn't return, nor water. So he began to
search. He also came to the lake and found that
ominous bird standing there. The stork said, 'King,
you must not drink any water until you have answered
my questions. If you answer my questions rightly, you
can drink. I also promise that your brothers will come
back to life.' So the king said, 'O bird, ask these
questions.' The stork asked lots of questions, several
scores of questions, and the king gave all the right
answers. Several of these questions and their answers
have become very famous; they are quoted in and out
of season. And one of them I shall quote now: 'What
is the greatest wonder, greatest surprise in this world?'
The king answered: 'Every day beings are dying and
entering into the house of death, and all those who
remain behind think they will remain permanently
here. What can be more surprising than that?'

We should ask ourselves this question. I spoke of a
pervasive ignorance. You see how ignorant we are that
we hold on to this stupid and foolish idea! Everything
is in a flux. Body is in a flux; we have no control
over it. Age comes, disease comes, death comes

inevitably; yet our whole scheme of existence is based on the idea that everything will be permanent. There is this ignorance; but, you see, however ignorant the behaviour in which we indulge, we *have* a sense of permanence; there is this nagging feeling that we are seeking something eternal. All religions and all philosophies worthy of the name have tried to find this one permanent reality. That is one side of our pursuit: We have to pass through everything that is perishable, insubstantial, unreal; we have to reach the bedrock of that which never changes, the eternal.

But that pursuit does not always give complete satisfaction. Some people are born with a strong philosophical sense; they cannot ignore any value or any truth. If they find even a little fragment of truth, they cannot ignore it. Some people can ignore it; others cannot. So there is another pursuit. It would not be enough to find this eternal Being; you must also explain the existence of many souls, of body, of mind, of the physical world and of other kinds of worlds – all of those things you want to account for, and all of them you trace to this one Being, this one eternal Reality. When you have done that, you may say that your quest for truth has ended; you have found that by knowing which everything else becomes known. Swami Vivekananda often used to quote that sentence from the Upanishads: *kasmin nu bhagavo vijñāte sarvam idam vijñātam bhavati* [1] – 'Sir, what is that by

---

[1.] *Muṇḍaka Upaniṣad*, 1. 1. 3.

knowing which everything else becomes known?' If you read the old books of Vedanta you will find that the age of the Upanishads was a glorious period when innumerable men and women set out on the journey of the Spirit, trying to find that by knowing which everything becomes known. That is the monistic quest.

Well, some of you might say, 'That's awfully nice of these old philosophers, but not all of us have to make that quest.' You might say that, but you know, you can't escape it. A time comes when something within us wakes up and asks, 'What am I doing?' Such questions come. Our idea in India is that the soul can go through only so much worldly experience and no more. It gets fed up with those things. Literally fed up. It no longer has any stomach for worldly experience; it turns away in disgust from everything in which the mind has been indulging. To every soul will come that day, that blessed day. From one point of view you might say it's a most disastrous day; from another, I say it is a blessed day. And when that day comes, the quest for eternal Reality will become an obsession with you; you won't be able to escape it.

What I am saying is that the pursuit of the monistic ideal with earnestness, or of any spiritual ideal, is not given at any time to everyone. Religion is not for everyone. Now, that's a strange thing to say, because, generally, religious people want to say that religion is for everybody — only, some people are a bit perverse; all that is required is just a little persuasion to make them see things rightly, then they will become religious. We don't believe it. We believe that only when a person reaches a certain stage of evolution where small things don't matter any more will he or she become religious. The soul says, 'I don't want to be rich. What is there in that for me? I do not want things of the senses. There is nothing in them for me. I don't care whether people call me famous or not. I don't care for all those things. I care for the goodness of God. He is the source of infinite joy and sweetness and love, and I want to come close to Him and live close to Him.' To worldly people that seems madness. To that person worldly people appear mad—completely mad. And that is the true fact about religion. *Yā niśā sarvabhūtānām tasyām jāgarti samyamī* [2] — 'In that which all beings are as it were steeped in night, the night of ignorance, there the man of self-control is awake.' No, religion is not for all, but it will be for everyone at one time or another. If you ask, 'Then why preach religion?' this is why: Say someone has a little awakening within him; if you stimulate it, it can become stronger and better and larger. If you blow rightly at a spark of fire, you can make it burn brighter and brighter until it bursts into a real blaze. You can do that, but the spark must be there; the fire won't burn until one has seen through this so-called reality. In other words, you could say that monism is a spiritual or philosophical view that will appeal only to people in whom there is a hunger

---

2. *Bhagavad-Gītā*, 2. 69.

for the one eternal Reality, which is the essence of everything that is and which is the sole explanation of everything. Let me explain this point.

2

Among the holders of these different views — the dualistic, the pluralistic, the qualified monistic, even the monistic (although I consider the last to be pseudomonists) — there are some who maintain that a person holds a certain view according to his temperament. For instance, one who is devotional in his heart would like to be a dualist or a qualified monist; he would not like to be a monist, because monism, as you must have understood, implies that the distinction between the soul and God can no longer remain; all become one. Many there are who do not like this self-absorption in God. Some say, 'What is the benefit of that in which I lose my own consciousness? If I become one with God, I will no longer be a separate entity. After all these struggles, in the end I just die!' It is as if a person had been searching for vast wealth and eventually discovered a treasure, but the moment he touched it he died. What good were all those years of search, what good his finding this treasure? No good. Some have taken that view; they have said they like to remain distinct and separate from God and love Him eternally. Or there are some who are so conscious of the majesty and lordship of God that it is very difficult for them to think there is even a basic unity between themselves and God. They feel that the soul, this individual man, is utterly separate from God; God is the Creator and he is a creature, and creature and Creator can never be one in any sense. In itself the soul has not the power to see God or attain to that state of beatitude. But through His grace God grants something to the soul at the proper time, and with the help of that, the soul can have the vision of God. Those are dualistic views.

There are of course various versions of dualism in different religions, but they all have more or less the same idea: there is no connection between God and the soul so far as essence is concerned. Those who like this view think of God as the Lord, the Giver of gifts, the Protector. He is infinitely more powerful than the most powerful individual on earth; He is the Lord of all time, of all laws, of all space, of all forms; all things that happen, happen according to His wish; He is the Giver of rewards as well as punishments. Such devotees generally take the attitude, 'I am Thy servant, O Lord, Thou art my Master. Grant me that I may serve You faithfully, that I may have the privilege of serving You.'

Others feel a little closer to God; they like the qualified monistic view. They want to remain distinct, and yet they recognize a basic connection between themselves and God, as son and father, as friends; sometimes they take the attitude 'God is my child'. You see how temperament plays its part. The differences in ideals are determined by the differences in the temperaments of the people who are seeking God. All these ideals are equally valid. That's one idea.

Another idea is that, allowing for all these differences of temperament and so on, there is a gradation of experience. You see, devotees do not know what will happen to them when their realization of God becomes extremely intense. It has been found in the lives of devotional mystics that there have been periods in which they became so much at one with God in the intensity of their love that they did not have distinct consciousness left in them. Monists ask them, 'Brother, wasn't that a monistic experience? When all distinctions and differences were wiped out, could you say that you perceived God at that time?' 'No, I couldn't say that, because the perceiver himself was gone; I was lost in Him.' 'Well, what was He like?' 'Oh, most exquisite, most exquisite! This is all I can say—just incomparable! That is all I can say, nothing more.' The monists have concluded that devotional mystics are just stubborn people; they deny their own experience. They had the monistic experience, but they won't try to explain it. They will say, 'I just swooned away in love. I just lost myself in God', but they don't understand what they are talking about. Of course, devotees are emotional, you must admit that, and they do not want to be too logical or thoughtful; but however that may be, there is the philosophical view that as dualists and qualified monists reach higher and higher states of realization, eventually they will all end in the realization of monism.

Now, I myself like to sit on the fence in this regard. Sometimes I agree that according to different temperaments there are different isms. At other times I become bold and I say no, all of them will end in monism, and I think I incline more often to this latter view. Still, nobody likes anything second best, and lest you think this view implies that to be a devotee is something less than the highest, I should tell you one reason I incline towards it.

You see, philosophy has often been written and studied in terms of reason; you might say there is no other way of finding truth. But there are other ways. There is the way of poetry, for example. What a poet writes sometimes doesn't make any meaning if you are too literal about it. There is no logical analysis possible; if you try to analyse poetry, you will ruin it. But through poetry profound truths can be brought home to you, sweetly and beautifully. So, you see, there is that other way, the way of poetry. Through music, through all art we reach some truths, just as through the exercise of reason we arrive at certain truths. I sometimes think the language of art is more effective. Logic may point to truth, but art not only points to it but can make you feel it. One defect about art, however, is that it is a language of hints and signs. You cannot argue with anyone about hints and signs, and therefore the language of art has never been accepted as the language of persuasion. If you want to persuade another person and hold him to something definite, you have to use the language of reason; philosophy, therefore, has always taken to that language. And since monism is essentially the path of philosophy, it has been presented more often than not in the language of reason. Because of that, the conclusion has been that only through reason can a person attain to monism. I thoroughly disagree with that view. In persuading another person or writing a persuasive thesis — that is to say, a thesis which will appeal to reason — I may have to use the language of reason; but if I want to understand monism for myself, I can use the language of the heart as well as the language of the head. In other words, if you are temperamentally so suited that you reach towards love, towards beauty, then your heart can reach towards God, as in dualism, and yet your ideal can be monistic. That is to say, you can approach the monistic ideal — at-onement with God — also through the heart, through love.

But just as in the path of reason you must be alert to see that there is no logical error anywhere, because that will be the death of reasoning — one little logical error made somewhere will extend through the subsequent arguments and vitiate all of them — so in the path of love there is a defect you must also watch for. Do you know what is poison to love? Selfishness. And that goes for all kinds of love. Wherever there is a suspicion of one's holding one's self or one's own interest from the other, love is vitiated. Therefore in the path of love, whether human or divine, we should be completely wary that no selfishness creeps in. *Selflessness* is the watchword.

Now, let us suppose a devotee says, 'I don't want anything for myself, I want to be lost in God.' At that moment he can attain to the monistic ideal. It is our selfishness which holds us away from this great truth. 'I have my own interests, I think in a certain way.' Suppose the Lord comes to a person and says, 'Now, look here. You want Me, you say? If you want Me you should not have all your own things; these are like a barrier between you and Me.' 'Lord, I just cannot help it. I cannot give up these things. You should not ask too much of me.' The Lord will say, 'Very good, be My distant devotee — from several miles off.' But the more that person gives up, the less he has for himself, the closer he comes to God. Barriers become thinner and thinner until all barriers are gone between the soul and God. That is monism. I say therefore that it is also possible to realize the monistic ideal through love. And when I think that it can be realized either through reasoning or through love, I am inclined to think that the path of the dualist or the qualified monist remains incomplete until it has ended in this incomparable Love, indescribable Love, which is the same thing as Consciousness.

Well, the Indian sages reached that conclusion long, long ago. It must have been the most glorious day in the history of man when an ancient seer first burst upon this truth. Like a river starting from a very distant fastness of a mountain, trickling its way down, cutting its way through mountains and all kinds of obstructions, winding and winding, and at last reaching a point where it bursts into the sea, the heart of man must have come through all kinds of difficulties and misconceptions and unknown territories to this grand realization in which the human spirit loses itself in the divine Spirit. No doubt there is a date and an hour to that, but of course the date and hour are lost; we only know of that age, several thousand years before Christ, when the Hindu people became crazed over the idea of oneness with God. We are most proud of that period of our history, because it is so unique; no other nation has devoted itself to the realization of truth to that extent. In a small measure there was a similar period in the history of Christianity in the first centuries after Christ, when a sort of compulsion came upon many Christian devotees to go into the desert and search for God through contemplation and asceticism. They were seized with that mania. That was the time when Christianity acquired its strength — the strength by which it is being sustained even now. Just as through geological epochs vast lakes were formed underground so that for thousands of years thereafter springs have spurted cool water, in the same way religions gathered strength in distant ages, and afterwards through centuries and centuries people are sustained by this strength which comes in driblets here and there.

Such was that glorious period in Indian history: those ancient sages didn't want to remain even one inch separated from this grand and ultimate Truth. As long as there remained even a suspicion of time, they were unconsoled; they wanted to go beyond time. They would not brook any condition. No wonder they have called this state of realization *freedom, liberation*. We don't call it salvation, or attainment of the kingdom of heaven, or any such thing. We say *freedom — mukti* or *moksa*. You feel now that you are bound; you, the free, eternal, immortal, infinite Being, are hemmed in by all kinds of bondages. When you become conscious of it, you strain against even the least bondage until you have become completely free. Like that, the soul reaches this goal. That is called monism.

Monism implies naturally two concepts: One is the unreality of the material world, including our body and mind. Very drastic. And the other is that I, the individual, am truly the universal God. In Sanskrit this second concept is expressed in various ways, such as *so 'ham*,[3] 'I am He'; *tattvam asi*,[4] 'That thou art'; *aham brahmāsmi*,[5] 'I am Brahman'. Such sentences are called *mahāvākyas*, supreme statements, because they contain the highest truth, the grand conclusions of monism. Many Hindus continually recite these grand truths and think about them.

But that is not enough. As I said before, these ideals are realizable, that is to say, they can become actual

---

[3.] e.g., *Chāndogya Upaniṣad*, 4. 11. 1.

[4.] *Chāndogya Upaniṣad*, 6. 8. 7.

[5.] *Bṛhadāraṇyaka Upaniṣad*, 1. 4. 10.

facts of our experience. If you do not experience them, they are not much good to you. Of course, I admit that since I have a mind and have to think of something, it is much better that I think of myself as Spirit, of the same nature as God, than that I think of myself as a mortal being, embodied. I admit that. But our goal is much higher, much greater, and therefore we shall not remain satisfied with only thinking about those things, we would like to experience them.

Would you not like to experience that you are deathless? Then you would not have any fear. And about those whom you love you can think, 'No, even if they die they have not died'. What a great consolation it would be to know that even if the body becomes old, you are not old. You might say, 'Well, I may say that, but I am old anyhow'. No, it is said that you are as young as you feel; there is a great deal of truth in that. Of course, you can also understand it in a very stupid way: there are some old fools who behave like young fools. I do not mean it in that sense; I mean it in the sense of being unaffected by the conditions of the body and by the conditions of the mind that follow upon the decay of the body, in the sense that your perceptions remain unimpeded by bodily or mental conditions, in the sense that you become aware of something which is beyond the body and the mind. Don't you think *that* kind of youthfulness, that kind of feeling would be very welcome? And you can have it.

Meanwhile, so many benefits can come just from practising this basic monism! For instance, if you are a devotee of God you could look at the face of God and say, 'I am one with You! Even though You might appear now a million miles distant, You are still bound up with me because You are the Soul of my soul; You cannot get away from me.' Just imagine having that sort of thought! We have our hours of despair, our hours of failure, and if we give way to those things, they can create havoc in our spiritual life. If we get the idea that we have been forsaken by God, what terrible misery it would be! It is said that in his later life the English poet Cowper felt that he had been eternally forsaken by God, and he wrote a poem expressing that feeling. I read that poem long ago and felt the pathos of it. Well, some people feel like that. But monism will rescue them. Suppose a person has done all kinds of wrong things and now wants to follow the truth. What would he do? Sit in sackcloth and ashes and tear his hair and beat his breast? Repent? What good would that do him? Where would be the strength by which he could climb back? Monism gives him that strength. It is not a false strength; it is based on the recognition of facts.

The facts are these: If I am the Spirit, if body and mind are unreal, then whatever may have happened regarding them could not be real. Even in my utmost degradation I know I have the pristine purity of my nature, my divine nature. And if I remind myself of that fact, it will become my strength. When there is nothing to depend on in the outside world, when no strength is given by your body or by your mind, when no assurance comes from the gods or from God, there is still one source of strength, and that is your own Self. You can always count on that. You can say, 'No. In me is infinite strength, I am the infinite One, I am the eternal One. Let the whole stellar universe break down on my head, I will not be crushed by it!' You can stand upon this, whatever might happen to you. Life *is* a burden. I am not saying that in a pessimistic sense; I am just recognizing it. Many are the burdens we have to carry, but if we know we have invincible strength, inexhaustible strength within us, we won't be overwhelmed by these burdens. That's the negative benefit of monism.

The positive benefit is this: We are all dreaming a beautiful dream of realizing wonderful things; that is what we are all about. We go to school, we marry, we beget children, we make friends, we earn money, we want to achieve name and fame. What for? Because there is somewhere a beautiful dream. We don't know even the outlines of that dream, but there *is* a dream, and we are eager to realize it. But never can you realize it in the outside. Even if you were to realize it for a moment, the next moment everything would be broken up. It is as if you were writing on moving water. Before you can draw a line even a quarter of an inch long, it has disappeared. But there is one place where this dream can be realized, and that is in the Spirit, which you are, which I am, which everybody is.

I could go on endlessly telling you of the benefits of this monistic attitude and of the realization of the monistic vision. But then you would all say: 'Wonderful, wonderful, but it is very difficult to realize. It is like a poor man who thinks about what he could do if he had millions. He draws all kinds of plans for palaces and parks, but he hasn't even five hundred dollars; so all this planning is useless labour.' You would tell me that. Therefore I should tell you some of the things you can practise.

3

If you agree with me that monism can be practised from the devotional as well as the philosophical point of view — then I must tell you that you can put some of these things into practice *now*. Once in course of a lecture in Madras in 1897 Swami Vivekananda said, 'Be strong. Believe you are this infinitely powerful Spirit. Believe it. If you believe in this and if you are a fisherman you will be a better fisherman. If you are a lawyer you will be a better lawyer. Everything you do, you will do better.'[6] You have a part of this teaching in some of your modern doctrines. For example, Christian Scientists want to take the attitude that everything is perfect. They say death is not, disease is not, and they are helped by that thought. I say why not? If I have to think, why should I not think correct thoughts? Why in the name of any ism do I have to think I am a miserable sinner? The world

------

[6.] *Complete Works of Swami Vivekananda*, 3: 244-45.

has held such negative thoughts for ages and ages; the world has remained the same. It is time we try to think more positive thoughts.

Let us affirm within ourselves under all conditions, 'I am this infinite Spirit. I am still under the influence of ignorance, I am groggy, it is true, but that's not my natural state. My natural state is strong. Even if my mind does not feel devotion for God now, what difference does it make? If God seems far off, I won't accept that, because that is not the truth. It is just a question of time before the tide will turn and I shall think, God is the Soul of my soul. Lord, however low I may have sunk, You will not leave me, because you *cannot* leave me. I am a part of Your being, one with You, You are one with me forever, from eternity to eternity.' Now, just consider, would not this affirmation be a tremendous stimulant to your practice of devotion? That's the monistic spirit. Whatever the doctrine, whatever the philosophical presentation of it, that is the spirit of monism. In other words, in everything, in worldly life or intellectual life, as well as in spiritual life, the practice of monism will give you strength and courage and optimism. And there is no reason why it should not be very widely practised.

Swami Vivekananda said, whatever you do, do it like a strong man. Don't ever be like a small man. Don't be a sneak thief. If you want to loot, loot the treasury of the king, and if you want to hunt, hunt the rhinoceros; that's the motto. If you want worldly things, aim high and do nobly there; don't follow the sneaky path. If you want to be rich, be rich, exercising your intelligence in an honest way, aboveboard. He would advise that. Have infinite strength and faith in yourself! If you want to enjoy life, enjoy life like a strong man.

Then comes a stage in which you want to realize the spiritual ideal from this monistic viewpoint. There your path might be that of reason or of action or of concentration or of devotion, it doesn't matter; the thing to practise is nonidentification with the body and the mind. You say, I am not this body, I am not this mind. Of course, I admit that just saying so won't do. In this stage, these affirmations must be accompanied by actual practice. Here also the advice is, be a strong soul. The violation of your internal word by your external behaviour just weakens you, takes all the courage out of you. If a man thinks something to be true but does not carry out his belief, if he belies his internal truth by his outward action, then he undermines himself. So the two have to go together. If the body is not real, the hungers of the body are not real, appetites of the senses are not real, the vagaries of the mind are not real. We find out the source of all those illusions and cut at their root with the sharp knife of reason. *Knife* did I say? *Sword* I should say. Nothing less than a sword will do —wielded by a powerful hand. We shall cut at the root of all these stupidities. In this second stage we do that; we say, 'Enough of this, I have had enough of this world; I no longer want these corroding things. Now I am for higher things; let not the body and the mind stand in my way.' You become a fire and burn the stupidities of body and mind; or you wield the powerful sword of reason and analysis and cut them at the very root. You find your body has separated from you. Outwardly it may not be so noticeable. There will be the same body; yet those who have the eyes can discern certain signs by which they can recognize that the body is not sticking to a person like glue; it has separated. The things of the body cannot influence or affect him; the senses cannot trouble him; nor do many thoughts and desires rise in his mind. They have all become uprooted, and there comes a serenity in him. Although you talk with him, and he responds like any other person, if you are observant you will notice that a part of his mind is somewhere else, as it were. A part of his mind has become aware of the presence of this one vast Spirit, which in our ignorance we call God and in our knowledge we call Self. Some of you are ready to practise these things, and to the extent that you practise, to that extent you will achieve.

And why should you not practise this? You are all lords and ladies honourable. If someone says you are good for nothing, you will flare up. But all the time you are telling *yourself* that you are good for nothing. If I ask you, 'Why can you not practise these things in the search of truth?' you say, 'Oh, that's not for me, I am not ready for it'. You mean you are good for nothing, don't you? You are saying to yourself that you are a weakling. Why should you do that to yourself?

Why? Do you think only little things are to be attained in life? There is a saying in Bengal that the domestic cat, that mewing cat, will become a snarling and growling bobcat when he goes into the woods. In other words, when this very man, feeling insignificant, helpless, attains to even a little truth he becomes like a lion.

You remember that most beautiful story that the monists tell of the lamb-lion? We are all lamb-lions. It seems a lioness in the fullness of her time fell upon a flock of sheep and in that exertion gave birth to a cub and died. Well, the cub grew amongst the sheep, who licked it and nursed it and so on. Of course the lion cub didn't know it was lion; it grew amongst these lambs and became big and learned to eat grass and to bleat. Then in course of time another lion came by and was astonished to see a full-grown lion grazing amongst sheep. When he approached the flock, all of them, including the lion, ran away, and that young lion began to bleat. The stranger lion was awfully surprised to see the degraded condition of his fellow creature. So he bided his time, and one day he grasped him. Of course the lamb-lion bleated in fear, 'Don't kill me!' So he shook him, 'What are you saying? You are a lion!' 'Oh, no, no, I am not a lion, I am a lamb, a poor lamb. Please don't hurt me.' So the lion dragged him to the side of a pool and said, 'Look at your reflection; look at mine! You see that?' Of course he found that both were the same. 'Ye-ess.' 'All right!' So he brought some raw meat and put it into his mouth,

'Eat this!' And the lamb-lion tasted blood. 'Now roar!' So he began to roar. 'Come on with me to the woods; you are a lion!'

They tell us these stories in monistic philosophy. Again, you sometimes hear or read in the pages of history that amongst a subjugated people a great man arose and made his country independent. If he had behaved like his fellow beings they would all have remained oppressed, and he one of them. You notice that those who liberate their people don't accept the prevailing conditions. For instance, there was Shivaji. He was born in the seventeenth century during the reign of Aurangzeb, the last of the great Moguls who reigned at Delhi. Aurangzeb was a most extraordinary man, very clever, very industrious, very diligent, very ascetic. But one thing ruined him — he had a crooked heart, he never trusted anybody, and he was a fanatic. Those are three things, but all three are really one: they follow from a smallness of nature. However, during his reign the Mogul empire reached its greatest extent. Shivaji was born in central India, in a state called Maharashtra, a mountainous country. His father was an important officer in the service of the Moguls, and his mother, whom he adored, was very devout. Of course, the father was always away, going from this place to that, and so the training of the boy was left to the mother and an old brahmin servant in the family. They taught him all the heroic stories of the *Rāmāyaṇa* and the *Mahābhārata*. Well, many people have learned these stories and very little change has been brought about in them, but Shivaji looked around himself and said, 'Why do we have to bow down to the Mohammedans? Why do they say, "Do this, and do that", and persecute us? Why can we not do anything about it?' Of course his mother would tell him, 'Now, don't say such things! The Mogul empire is very powerful. You be obedient.' He would not accept that. He was a born leader. All the boys of all castes in the whole community became his followers, and in play he used to drill them, as boys do. But this fire was in him: he wouldn't accept the situation. Word went about that the boy was saying all kinds of treasonous things, and the Mogul officers began to ask the father, 'What kind of boy are you training?' The father was of course embarrassed and scolded his son, but it made no difference. Well, this is the man who practically broke up the Mogul empire and established a huge kingdom of his own.

Yes, that is the way, my friends: if we accept the prevailing conditions at their face value, then we live under the heel of the Moguls. But do we have to accept them? Why do you accept all these conditions? They are not true. If they were true, I would say of course you have to accept them. But none of these conditions are true. You are not the body, you are not the mind; the things that you are pursuing are unreal. Why should you remain a slave to falsehood? So I say look to the truth, and you will become a singular person; you will establish a kingdom of your own.

We have a word for it: the highest state of realization is called *svarājya-siddhi*, 'attainment of self-government', or *sāmrājya-siddhi*, 'establishment of empire'. You are the emperor, the whole universe is your empire. That is what the monists say.

And why not? Monism above all demands of us that we think and feel not cravenly but courageously, heroically. It demands that we never be satisfied with anything small. *Nāyam ātmā balahīnena labhyaḥ* [7] 'This Self cannot be attained by one who is devoid of strength.' *Nālpe sukham asti, bhūmaiva sukham* [8] 'In the small, in the limited there is no happiness; the vast alone is happiness.' That's it.

---

[7] *Muṇḍaka Upaniṣad*, 3. 2. 4.

[8] *Chāndogya Upaniṣad*, 7. 23.

THE RAZOR'S EDGE

1

Probably you are reminded by my subject of the title of a novel written by Somerset Maugham, *The Razor's Edge*. I have no doubt that this title was borrowed from the English translation of one of the verses of the *Kaṭha Upaniṣad: kṣurasya dhārā niśitā duratyayā; durgam pathastat kavayo vadanti*[1] – 'The sages say that the path to the realization of the Spirit is as sharp as the edge of the razor and very difficult to tread.'

There are similar statements in almost every religious literature of the world, and one that occurs immediately to us is Christ's saying, 'Strait is the gate, and narrow is the way.'[2] Of course, *strait* means narrow; both the path as well as the gate have been called narrow. And the reason the gate is called narrow is that in the beginning we rarely notice its existence.

---

[1]. *Kaṭha Upaniṣad*, 1. 3. 14.

[2]. Matthew, 7: 13-14.

Isn't it true? If we look around ourselves, one of the most disheartening things is that there is no door to where God dwells. Whichever way we look we come across only material phenomena. When we look outside there is this universe, the object of the senses, which oftentimes bewilders us and tempts us and certainly stands as an insurmountable barrier to the realm of the Spirit. And when we look within there is this turbulent mind, continually changing in its thoughts and activities. And if we want to grasp the centre of these mental activities, which is the ego, we find it very difficult to put our finger on it. Of course, we always sense our 'I', and we are rarely proud of it, but even when it is behaving well or presenting a pleasant face, we feel that it could not be the Spirit or the Self which we are seeking. Everywhere, therefore, we find that there is no gate to the realm of the Spirit, no door wide open. Yet there must be a door somewhere; otherwise, how can we go beyond this world of the senses and of ordinary thought and enter into the realm of God? But that gate is so narrow that it is invisible. You really cannot see it.

And as to the path, when you have entered the gate and started along the path, you find no royal highway there. It looks like a lost trail, and you wonder whether it will lead you anywhere at all. Rightly, therefore, these expressions have been used – the gate is narrow and the way itself is also narrow. I must add here that if the full story of the way had been told, it would have been said that as we proceed along that pathless path we shall gradually come upon a well-marked and very broad highway indeed, and the City of God, also, will not remain invisible; it will be seen, though it be from a very great distance, shining against the horizon. Well, that is the story. Why is it so, and how are we to tackle this present disheartening situation? These are the questions I would like to dwell upon.

No great teacher has ever told us that the way to God-realization is easy. Nor have any said that with a little effort we shall see the face of God. I know these are very discouraging statements; the tendency nowadays is to say that God is at our beck and call; all we have to do is press certain buttons, and God will come at once like a most obedient servant. In various ways things are made very alluring to us, and I must say that if you listen to a few of our lectures here, I think you will also go away with the idea that to realize God is pretty easy. But when you read our literature, you don't get that idea. You find that all kinds of difficulties are to be overcome, and all kinds of rules and disciplines are to be observed – things to be done and things to be avoided – before we can expect to come to the realization of God. If you want to have a vivid understanding of what God-realization involves, I shall recommend the study of *The Gospel of Sri Ramakrishna*. There is also another very large book, *Sri Ramakrishna the Great Master*, by one of his direct monastic disciples. Both these books originally were written in Bengali and are of course available in English translation. In the *Gospel*, through the conversations of the Master, and in the *Great Master*, through the explanations and delineations of the author, you vividly see the reality of spiritual life, spiritual struggle, and spiritual attainment, and you understand what tremendous alertness has to be observed in order to make any gain in this path.

Now, you might well ask why it is so difficult. When we speak in terms of monistic Vedanta, we say that God is everywhere, God is here and now, ever present; moreover, God is already within our own heart. And when we go further on in monistic Vedanta, we say that in its true nature everything *is* God, I also am God, my true nature is God. Then we go still further and say there is nothing else than God; even when we think we are perceiving other objects, it is really God whom we are perceiving, only we are perceiving Him mistakenly. Further, we say that in one moment, or a fraction of a moment, the veil of *māyā* can drop away and we can at once have the supernal vision. All these things we say. But we do *not* say that this sudden illumination should happen naturally and as a matter of course to everyone. In other words, it is not promised to everyone. It *may* happen, that's the idea; or, to use devotional language, it happens by the grace of God.

The grace of God cannot be earned; it is conferred by God upon us; if we could earn it, then it would be the result of effort on our part; it would be governed by law, and therefore it could not properly be called grace. But notice this, in devotional religions we are told that it is *possible* to have the grace of God, and there are stories about how so and so became transformed overnight. These stories are true. Sri Ramakrishna sometimes used to give illustrations of divine grace; he would say, suppose a very poor man receives a letter from an attorney which says a certain distant cousin has left him a vast fortune. Overnight he becomes a rich man. From poverty to riches in just one step, with no effort on his part. He also used to speak of grace in a somewhat different way. He would say suppose a man is digging in his yard and uncovers a hidden spring, and suddenly water gushes out. Similarly God-realization can suddenly come. But mind, no religion ever tells you that it *must* come at a certain time of your spiritual life. They never will tell you that.

So what do you do? If you are following a theistic religion, you go on daily practising devotion. In India that kind of practice is called *vaidhī* devotion—that is to say, according to *vidhi*, rules or disciplines. There are practices that bring certain results: your mind and heart will become purified; you begin to have a liking for God, you like to think about Him, you like to hear about Him or speak about Him, you like to sing His glory. All these things naturally come, and after a time you find you have developed a longing for God. From that point on, you enter into the true spirit of devotion. If in the meantime the grace of God comes to you, so much the better. And, as I said, it does sometimes come. I myself have met people to whom it has come; so I am compelled to believe that such a thing can happen.

Now, this possibility of grace accords with our philosophy of monistic Vedanta: since the Spirit, which God is and which we always are, is our true nature, there is a certain indefiniteness about when it will break out in all its glory and might. But if it doesn't break out, then we do not sit still, we undergo practices. You see, something which does not happen according to rule is very unpredictable. The moment we consider that fact, we see innumerable difficulties in the path. The mind with which we would seek God, even that mind is itself distorted. There was a saint who used to write beautiful songs, in one of which he said, 'Mother, You have winked at the mind, and the mind has turned toward the world.' The Divine Mother has given a certain impetus to the mind, has given it an outward direction. In one of the Upanishads it is said, 'Providence has so made the senses that they always go outward instead of seeing the Self within, but some people, desiring to see the Self within, turn their senses inward.'[3] Some make that effort, but the natural tendency of the senses and the mind is to go outward.

Well, I am piling difficulty on difficulty in the elaboration of my theme, and I hope I will not

---

[3.] *Kaṭha Upaniṣad*, 2. 1. 1.

discourage you too much by this kind of talk. Why should you feel discouraged? On the other hand, why should you be unnaturally encouraged? Neither reaction befits a strong soul. And you must remember that whatever path you follow you can never find a substitute for strength. Many people think one religion is very difficult and another is easy. That could be true only in the sense that the 'easy' religion is more in keeping with one's own temperament. One feels more at home in it; therefore it does not seem so difficult — just as we can easily speak the language we are born in. But one should not conclude that just because we feel at home in a certain religion its path will always be easy for us. When we have to take further steps, there will be struggle. One must be ready for that; therefore one has to embrace the life of religion with strength and not with weakness. Always and everywhere quiet, persistent strength is the answer. There is no substitute for it. All the tall talk we hear: 'Take refuge in God, everything will be all right' — such talk, I sometimes think, is just self-deceived and deceiving conversation.

You see, whenever we think that God will do something for us, that we don't have to worry about it, when we look back, we find we have been saddled with the tremendous obligation of giving up all initiative of our own; in everything we have had to become reliant on God. People speak of self-surrender! 'We don't have to do anything; we shall surrender ourselves to God, God will do it for us.'

You think it is easy? As long as we have a desire of our own, as long as we have all these turbulent senses, which we call our senses, as long as we say 'I see, I hear, I think, I want' — as long as we have these notions, do you think we can surrender ourselves to God? You might ask, 'Then what are the teachers talking about when they speak of self-surrender?' They are speaking of it as a practice, an effort. In everything we should make an effort to say, 'No, let Him do it; not I, but Thou'. Whenever we find that we go ahead with our own self-assertion and self-will, this practice of self-surrender makes us stop and say, 'No, let His will be done'. And we pray to Him, 'Make me do things as You will, not as I will.' And of course eventually we have to give up all our own personal will. We have to learn to say to ourselves, 'I don't want anything. It is as You want.' 'Don't you have any preferences of your own?' 'No, Lord, I haven't any preference; whatever You want me to do I shall do.' That is how it happens. But before we reach this state of complete self-surrender, complete self-abnegation, where no longer any self remains to call our own, we have passed through a lot of stages and a lot of struggle.

Now, in the Upanishads the road has been called 'sharp as the edge of a razor'. What is the significance of this? Since the road is also said to be *duratyayā*, 'very difficult to tread', you almost have a picture in your mind of someone actually walking on a razor's edge. Or it might mean that a razor's edge is so very fine that if, when shaving, you hold your razor at a slightly wrong angle, you will make a gash: it's altogether a bloody affair, you see. That could be one of the meanings. Generally, however, the verse is said to mean that the way is like *walking* on the sharp edge of a razor.

I have a vague memory of seeing something like this as a little boy. In the villages of Bengal there was a certain day in the last month of the year when people used to perform all kinds of ghastly but almost miraculous things. By their own mental powers they would make certain parts of their body insensitive. For example, they would put a hook under the spinal column and whirl on that hook. And after the hook was taken out, the wound would heal easily. You see, there was a period in India when people used to delight in practising hard asceticism; they would take a vow to live like great ascetics for a whole month and thereby they would generate these mental powers. Although in its extreme form asceticism has always been condemned, one cannot but admit that without it we become flabby, we have no vigour left within us. Therefore there should always be a touch of austerity in our existence. Physically, you all do that. You want to bathe in cold water; you want to go into snow; you know it is enervating to remain in heated rooms all the time. When we also treat the senses and the mind austerely, strength comes within them. Well, in the olden days in India people used to practise fasting, vigils, and so on. And as I said, on one day during the last month of the year they would demonstrate their powers. What I saw was probably the last vestige of these practices. I remember that two people held a long, sharp sword at its ends, and a man would stand barefoot on the edge of the blade and dance there without cutting his feet at all. Probably the explanation is that he maintained his balance very well, and that saved his feet from getting cut. Oftentimes when I have read this verse in the Upanishad I have remembered that childhood picture.

Yes, when we gain a certain balance in life, when the senses, the bodily forces, and the mind are balanced, then even in the midst of contrary circumstances we are able to proceed on; we do not get hurt. If we are unbalanced, we get hurt, we get cut. Probably that is what the author had in mind. Anyhow, it is enough for our purpose that he thought the spiritual path was very difficult to tread and that the utmost care should be taken in order to negotiate it successfully.

2

Where does this difficulty come from? And further, does everyone have to go through it? Here we can pinpoint certain facts about the spiritual path, and it will be helpful to recognize them, so that when anything untoward happens to us, we will be able to evaluate it rightly and not become unnecessarily discouraged.

To begin with, difficulties arise in spiritual life because we enter into it not properly prepared. You have all read, no doubt, many books on Vedanta or Yoga and you find the authors put things in a very nice, orderly fashion. They mention certain preliminary disciplines that are designed to bring our body, our senses, and our desires under our control, so that we attain to a state of purity and holiness. Although sensual, worldly desires may remain in a finer form, they do not arise to trouble us. The mind reaches a state of quietude and serenity in which we feel our closeness to God.

But the trouble about these rules is that even before we have fully acquired the virtues they speak of, our heart becomes eager to proceed along the path of the Spirit. We may not be fully disciplined; yet we would like to meditate. When you write systematically about a thing, it is very good to say: first practise this, then this and this, and then you will be ready for this — step after step. In actual life, however, it does not work out so well. Not that truth is not there; these steps do follow one after another. The Yoga system of Patanjali, for example, speaks of *aṣṭāṅga yoga*, that is to say, there are eight parts, the last four of which are the steps of meditation: *pratyāhāra*, *dhāraṇā*, *dhyāna*, and *samādhi*. *Pratyāhāra* means withdrawing the mind from things other than the Self or God. Then comes *dhāraṇā*, or holding your mind on the object of your meditation; you then learn to hold it there for a long time, and *dhāraṇā* becomes *dhyāna*, or meditation, as we translate it in English. Not only is *dhyāna* long and continuous, it has also to be profound: only in depth is continuity of meditation possible. So *dhyāna* becomes very deep and uninterrupted, and when it has become so well established that, if you want, you can continue indefinitely, you then realize — at an intense point — what is called *samādhi*. *Samādhi* is, really speaking, meditation at its highest.

Now, these are the four steps of meditation. But observe this peculiarity: meditation is actually one process. That is to say, you try to make your meditation more and more intense, more and more deep, and eventually you may realize *samādhi*. But from the beginning — withdrawing the mind from other things and holding it to God — meditation is what you want to achieve, better and better meditation. So these four steps are really parts of one process.

And when you think of the previous four steps, you find that they, too, are actually one process. The step immediately before *pratyāhāra*, or withdrawal of the mind, is *prāṇāyāma*. *Prāṇāyāma* means control of the breath or control of the vital energies. Why is it that these two — breath and vital energies — are used almost synonymously? Because you find that as your vital energy is, so is your breath. If your vitality is concerned with worldly things, your breath will be of one kind. If your vitality is concerned with spiritual things, your breath will be of another kind. By the breath of a person you can recognize in what state of mind he is, the two are so connected with one another. If for some reason your mind has withdrawn from the world, you will find your breath has become very long and very deep. Unconsciously it will change.

Sometimes when your mind is no longer concerned with worldly things your breath will completely stop. We call this state *kumbhaka*. *Kumbhaka* is a state where you feel no movement of air. Just as when you sink a full pitcher in a pool there is no movement of water in the pitcher itself, so in this state you no longer breathe in and breathe out. Some of you may say, 'Maybe if one becomes unconscious or some such thing breath can stop, but it is hard to believe that in a normal state it can happen.' Yes, it can happen, and it is a most wonderful state of relaxation and rest. You do not know what a burden we are carrying, this breathing machine. How much energy we have to spend in breathing in and out! Just because it is natural, don't think that it does not take a toll on our energy. It does. If you ever realize that state in which for some time you can go without breathing, you feel a wonderful rest. Of course, not having to spend energy in inhaling and exhaling is only part of it. You see, this state comes only when your mind has become calm, and that in itself will give you a sense of profound rest and quiet. Well, however that may be, we say that when vital energy has been brought under control, breath also has been brought under control. The word *prāṇāyāma*, therefore is oftentimes translated as breath control, although its inward meaning is control of vital energy, of which breathing is a manifestation.

You can well understand why vital energy has to be controlled. What is it that makes my eyes focus to see and my ears open up to hear? What is it that makes my hand go out to grasp? Vital energy, *prāṇa*, living energy. If this living energy were not behind the senses, the senses would not be active. You will say, 'We certainly want living energy behind our senses; otherwise we would be dead.' Yes, of course you want it, but you shouldn't have it when you *don't* want it. For example, if you don't want to listen to street noises, then this vital energy should not be behind your ears. But whether you want to hear or not, it is there. You cannot sleep because of noise. If you had control over your vital energy, you could withdraw it from your ears, and even if people were shouting all around you, you would feel peace and quiet. We don't want to see so many things, but that energy is behind our eyes, and whether we want it or not, it goes on functioning. That is where the problem lies.

About thoughts also — thoughts and emotions. Say whenever I look at someone I get annoyed. I just don't like the look of that person. Well, what is wrong with my feeling that way? If it were a conscious effort — here is the person, I am looking at him, the next step is to feel annoyed — that would not be so bad. You see, if I could do everything consciously, deliberately, then I could also say, 'No, I won't feel annoyed'. But our problem is that the moment our eyes have seen something, this reaction, this emotion rises, and there is no controlling it. Our vital energy is behind it. You might say, 'Vital energy is not at fault; the emotion itself is wrong'. That is true, but how do you control it? Suppose you find that heavy winter rains have dug a deep and dangerous trench just by your house. What are you going to do? First of all, you stop the water from flowing that way; you dam it somewhere; then afterwards, when it dries up, you can fill the trench. It will be very easy to control. But if the water flows continually and forcefully along that channel, how can you remedy anything? It will only get worse and worse. Similarly, when vital energy is in any thought or emotion or in any action of the body or the senses and we have no control of it, then there is danger. Our biggest work lies in bringing this *prāṇa* under control.

You know, some people react so quickly to things that they get into a way of thinking that some extraneous agent is acting upon them. That shows a very primitive state of mind; education ought to have remedied it. In India our whole approach is that whatever happens to me happens *because* of me. It is a very good principle. Say you go some place where the people look very rough and tough, and you say, 'Oh, such terrible people! My mind became filled with all kinds of ugly thoughts!' *They* are bad; so *you* have the ugly thoughts? The presumption is that you are good, and if you are right that they are bad, then *they* should have the ugly thoughts, not you. Let them carry their own burden. Why is it that you have the ugly thoughts? When we act on instinct, as animals do, that reaction is so swift we think some outside agency is making it happen. Gods or angels or devils are making things happen to us all the time. When good things happen we kneel down in gratitude to some invisible god and make offerings for his pleasure. If bad things happen, then we blame someone or something outside of us, and we run to somebody else for a remedy. But that is not right. It is *my* reaction that makes things happen. This approach has to be learned.

In India, because of our religious and philosophical background — I am talking particularly of the Hindus — we say 'If things happen to me it is because of my *karma*, the impressions I have acquired in the past'. *Karma* is not a mysterious force that has been imposed upon us by gods or demons. No. We say that our previous actions and experiences have left their impression on the mind and conditioned it; therefore we act and react in a certain way, and things happen to us in a certain way.

Swami Vivekananda once wrote to a disciple: If anything goes wrong around me or towards me, as a Vedantist I should ask this question of myself, why is it that I see evil in others or in my surroundings? It must be due to something in my own mind; otherwise, I would not even recognize evil.[4] And often in course of his lectures he used to give the illustration of a little child in a room with a bag of gold. A man comes

---

[4.] See *Complete Works of Swami Vivekananda*, 8: 383.

and takes that bag of gold. Would the child know that it is a theft? The child hasn't yet developed the idea of stealing; he couldn't recognize a theft. But if a grown-up man sees this bag of gold snatched away, he will know there is a theft and will raise a hue and cry about it. It clearly shows that the evil we see has something to do with our own mind. In India this is the way we are taught to think. I must not give you the idea that every Hindu consciously or very clearly feels this way, but that's our general tendency. I think in the West, too, you should deliberately learn this approach.

Nowadays you are told that you should not control your emotions too much or something will happen to your psyche and you will have to run to a psychiatrist. Now, I admit that if you have been brought up on pure emotion, if you have never been taught self-discipline, then too much restraint can be harmful. You see, you have fantastic ideas about child training. You think children should be allowed to express themselves. What would they express? What have they got within themselves that should be expressed either for their own edification or for the edification of others? You can go too far with this self-expression business. What you are forgetting is this: yes, self-expression we should have, there should not be self-suppression, but more than that, there should be self-realization. We have to build up good things before we express ourselves. Otherwise all of us talk, nobody knows anything; we just make noise. So first of all we should learn, and by discipline we should acquire restraint. If you teach children this discipline, as they grow up their reactions will not be instinctive. Well now, if we have grown up without learning self-control, no use regretting. The thing is to start learning it now. We should make our best effort to restrain our emotions.

One thing you have probably noted — you cannot take care of the mind piecemeal; you cannot do it. If you try to get rid of one mischief of the mind you will find other mischiefs have become strengthened. You have to work on all fronts at once. Go easy about it, but work on all fronts steadily. Worldly desires and emotions go hand in hand. If a person seeks the things of the world, things of the senses, you will find he is also very emotional. He becomes moody; if anything is said against him, for days he is under a cloud. All kinds of ugly feelings run through his heart; he cannot control them.

You have to say to yourself: 'The mind is not I, it is an instrument and I am going to straighten it. What I am has nothing to do with the state of my mind.' If you ask, 'What am I then? Am I something vacant or empty, if I am not the mind or the states of the mind?' Well, the scriptures all tell you what you are, but if you do not want to bother about the scriptures, try to feel that you are someone who is not mixed up with the states of the mind. Gradually learn to do that. That has been called the practice of detachment, *anāsakti*. Learn to become a witness, a *sākṣī*, a spectator of things; don't get mixed up with things;

remain calm and quiet and poised. You will feel a wonderful peace within you; there will occasionally come glimpses of your own existence, which is infinitely superior to any state of mind.

But let me repeat, you cannot realize this state if you give a free rein to your desires. You have to study them; you may find that some are dutiful, that is to say, they serve a good purpose. But even there you have to ask yourself how long you can go on fulfilling them. You will have to examine them from time to time, because what might have appeared good at one time may no longer appear good to you. It is all very well when you are a little child to play and break things, but when you have grown up, you cannot do that. So you have to examine your desires and slowly bring them under control.

Now, all energy has to function; it cannot be negated; it can only be redirected. So the moment you try to control your own personal desires, you have to create either a desire to do good to others, or a desire to realize God. Since a genuine desire to realize God is a far-off thing, there is the middle state where you conceive desires to perform noble acts. Noble acts are always unselfish, always for the good of others, for the service of others. You have to conceive them, and you have to direct your energies toward them. Any energy that is devoted to a good purpose becomes amenable; it is your friend. It does not go against you, nor do you have to control it as you have to control the energy that goes into the realization of your own selfish desires. That's the way your vital energies become purified and come under control. That is *prāṇāyāma*.

Before *prāṇāyāma* there is a step called *āsanam*. *Āsanam* means posture and, like *prāṇāyāma*, has been interpreted in a superficial way and in a deeper way. Superficially, it simply means a sitting posture. In India our yogis have cultivated innumerable such postures. Some of them are really extraordinary — the way they fold their legs and so on is certainly wonderful to look at. But in his *Yoga Sūtras* Patañjali himself says that all these postures are not necessary. He says, *sthira-sukham āsanam* [5] — 'Posture is that which is firm and pleasant.' In other words, the *āsanam* for you is that posture in which you can comfortably remain steady for a long time. The deeper meaning is that until you have learned to control your vital energies at least a little, until your mind has turned away from worldly things, this ability to sit calmly and quietly does not come to you. Yes, by external practices you can form some habits, but a natural posture where you can sit quietly, with a straight back, not moving much, that comes only when the mind is in balance. That is the deeper meaning.

How do you reach that state? Before *āsanam* there are two steps — *yama* and *niyama* — that involve all kinds of physical disciplines and also disciplines of the senses, the practice of moral virtues, and so on. So

---

[5.] *Yoga Sūtras,* 2. 46.

here we come to the beginning of the path.

3

Earlier I said one of the reasons we find the path so difficult is that we enter into it unprepared. And I said that in the books the way is given step by step, and everything looks systematic and appealing. There is justification for that approach; for example, if a person hasn't attained to some amount of *yama* and *niyama*, control of body and mind, it is in vain for him to practise *prāṇāyāma*, control over vital energies, or to try to meditate; he would have very little meditation. That much is true. But here is the catch: long before we have full control over our senses or our vital energies one part of the mind wants to meditate and is able to meditate — though not always and not fully or very successfully; still it likes to meditate and *can* meditate. So in actual practice you start all of these steps together. It is then that the difficulties arise.

You see, even in the beginning you may realize a very blessed state and find the whole universe filled to overflowing with God. Everything speaks of God. What an extraordinary thing! Even in memory you cannot think of worldly life and the worldly troubles you once had, and you wonder why you did not perceive this vivid presence of God before. Then through some mischance, you lose that state; you come down to earth, and it becomes difficult for you even to remember that there is such a thing as God. Such is *māyā*.

The word *māyā* is often used in our religious literature, and you know that in the monistic school of Vedanta it is used to indicate the philosophical fact of ignorance. But it is also used in many other ways. For instance, it is used to indicate this strange state of things: at one time I felt everything was God, and now it is almost impossible for me even to think that God exists. How can that be? Wherever I look, I see no sign of God, no sign of a door by which I could again enter into that blessed state; everything is blocked. That is *māyā*, a great piece of magic.

So what do we do? Through our higher instincts, through knowledge gathered from other people, through the direction of a teacher, or through the reading of holy books, and so on, we try somehow to find our way. Then it seems as if somewhere a little gate has opened. But when we enter, we find only a faint road, overgrown. We doubt that it is a road at all, or that we can go along it. We try, and oftentimes we fall. We try, as it were, to walk on the edge of a razor, and we cut our feet and fall down. That is part of the story.

Now, I shall again remind you: you have to be strong; you must be brave. There is no substitute for strength. When faintheartedness comes, you have to remind yourself that whenever you tackle the job of realizing this higher state of being, this higher knowledge, you will have to be brave and strong. Somehow we unconsciously think, and also many people tell us, that a time will come when the task will be very easy for us; so we should put it off until then. I, for myself, would not listen to that. The way is never easy; *always* you have to be strong; *always* you have to struggle. So when the mind protests, 'Oh, no, it is too much for me,' wisdom lies in saying, 'No, let me get the hard part over with!'

I used to say to myself, whenever some difficulty would arise, 'Well, I have to face it one day. If I put it off today, tomorrow I shall have to face it. Let me, then, get it over with today.' After all, you want to finish the difficult portions of your job first, don't you? So by various means you should hearten yourself. Then strength comes, and you find the way is not so difficult, after all. A balance comes into your being.

What is that balance? Balance is not only an alert sense that makes us aware of anything that is going even slightly wrong, it is also an immediate reaction whereby we remedy this situation. When we have that kind of alertness we become balanced. It is like the keen aesthetic sense of a great artist. When a line is wrong he will at once know it and correct it. Or if a great singer has sung a slightly sour note, others listening to him may not know anything is wrong — but it will grate on his ear and he will correct it. That kind of alertness is what we acquire through discipline.

Now, let me warn you about this: like everything else in this universe, the mind has its rhythm. Wherever there is energy, there is action and rhythm, up and down, up and down. The whole universe is a story of rhythm. Mental activity is energy; therefore it has its rhythms, its ups and downs. What are you to do about it? Nothing; you don't pay any attention to it. Let mental states come and go; *you* go steadily on, living according to certain rules and disciplines and plans. You just say, 'I shall practise like this every day; what does it matter whether I feel spontaneously hilarious today or whether I feel melancholy; what difference does it make? I shall call forth the best energies of my mind, I shall make the mind behave'. That is the attitude you should take towards the mind. You should not be the kind of person who gets cloudy when the sky is cloudy and has a big smile on his face when the sun shines. What kind of creature are you then? A piece of cloud can make you dance! You haven't any dignity or integrity of your own. Something happens, your mind becomes depressed, then you follow in the wake of the mind. Mind is gloomy; therefore you are gloomy. If I ask you why *you* should be gloomy just because your mind is gloomy, you probably will laugh at me. 'Look at this fellow! If my mind is down, am I not also down?' No, you are not! You certainly are not. That is the thing to be learnt in life.

I sometimes think that people who are out in the world learn a great deal about these things. In a sense they are in a more responsible position than those who are not in the world. Those not in the world tend to become self-centred; they become so selfish; they are keenly conscious of their little ills, their little difficulties. But when a person is in the world he cannot afford to think about those things. His body might be aching with flu; he still will have to put on his clothes and go out and work eight hours in the office. He is a responsible man and has to support his family; he really cannot pay attention to his ills or moods. He learns to go through the routine of life whether he is ill or well, whether his mind is amenable or not. In spiritual life, you have to take the same attitude; you must not allow the mind to become playful. You make it do what it should do. True, when the mind is down it will not do so well. What of it? You have to wrestle with it; it must be made to do what is expected of it. After a time you will find it does not go down so far. That habit has gone. Contrary conditions of mind may come, but you will realize they are not *your* condition, that you can still carry on your duties, your better thoughts, your meditations, and so on. Wrong thoughts come and go; they cannot affect you. A steadiness comes into the mind. That is how you become independent.

4

Well, when you have reached this state of independence from the mind, there comes another difficulty. I am not speaking here particularly of what in Christian mysticism has been called the dark night of the soul. And by the way, I would rather call it dark *nights* of the soul, because the condition they speak of occurs more than once during the life of the soul. Generally, Christian mystics say that you have illumination first, then you have a period of purgation, during which you have all kinds of troubles; then afterwards you attain union with God. But in India we say that what Christians call purgation is punctuated by good periods as well as bad; in every stage you will come upon days when you are wonderful and other days when you are down in gloom. That cannot be avoided, because, as I said, the mind has a tendency of moving up and down. But in that higher state that gloom is so superior to the happy days of our lower existence that generally others would not call it so very bad.

What I have in mind here, however, is this: when you have a considerable realization of God, when you have approached Him and have had some very extraordinary experiences of Him, there is a chance, unless you are very cautious and have very carefully observed all the rules of this life, that there may come a reaction. You hear of many a yogi or monk who lived an ascetic life for years and years and then suddenly changed. Our Puranas, those Sanskrit books that record stories of sages and saints, are full of tales about their falls. You see, in that high state the drama of life is played on a very vast stage. It is not the little things of life that take place there; we have gone beyond the bounds of an ordinary finite life, and we are now engaged in a tug of war between our highest realization and other mysterious forces because of which we originally were brought into this snare of phenomenal existence. If you have followed our philosophy, you will remember we say some primal force must have brought us into the realm of *māyā*, and that when we want to get out of *māyā*'s clutch and realize our infinite, eternal nature, our original nature, we have to give battle to that primal force, the primal force of ignorance. It is a battle that you are fighting in order to conquer the principle of time and space, of relative existence. And mind this: relative existence is not yours alone; it concerns the whole universe. So you are really fighting against the whole universe; you are defying the forces that have made this phenomenal world. Actually, there *are* forces that will bring you down. And here, again, one has to learn to maintain one's balance.

Well, the books and the teachers say that the one thing that can save a person from an adverse reaction in that high state is the cultivation of *vairāgyam*, dispassion. You start from a simple beginning, but you strengthen it and strengthen it as you go ahead. At every stage temptations will come — honour will come, fame will come, and when you have reached a very high state, psychic experiences and powers will also come for your enjoyment. In regard to all of them you practise *vairāgyam*. Sometimes people ask, 'Why should we not be interested in occult and psychic things? After all, they are a part of knowledge.' Yes, that sounds so very convincing as an argument, but like most of our knowledge here, that kind of knowledge is also for self-interest. When you have knowledge of those other worlds you find wonderful things there, and at once you become tempted. Just as knowing things here you become caught in their snare, similarly, knowing those finer things, you can become ensnared by them. But if you have practised dispassion all along, you will easily be able to reject them.

You see, in every stage there is a danger that we might lose our balance, and in every stage alertness has to be cultivated and practised. In the lower state we have many battles in the concrete world. In the higher plane we have battles against the subtle forces of ignorance. And if you have read Samkhya philosophy you will find that many souls, having almost attained that state in which the *Puruṣa*, or the Spirit, becomes free, at the last become charmed by the higher graces of *prakṛti*, or nature. You see, the nature that we see is the grossest part of this universe. There is a very fine part of the universe which is so attractive that even the very thought of it will make us weak, and those finer things are so vivid and real to a person that he may fall for them. The books call it a fall, although from our standpoint he is still in a most exalted state. Well, those are high things.

But the principle is always the same; therefore we should start cultivating balance and alertness from the very beginning. If we do it, we find that we have entered the narrow gate and are on the narrow road. Gradually that road widens, and we begin to see before us the goal we want to reach, the luminous City of God. We see it, and we know we are not far off from it.

off the outside world, then remaining serene all the time, and dwelling there and there — we all now that such meditation is impossible without a certain of the mind. Yet concentration is necessary to act. Although we have been trained from early childhood to pay attention to what we do, this paying attention which is nothing but the art of concentration, can be taught to.

MEDITATE WHILE YOU WORK: A
NEW PATH FOR A NEW AGE

1

There are certain spiritual practices that are universally recognized as such. Meditation, prayer, ritualistic worship, singing the praise of God — almost all religions have recommended these practices in one form or another for the attainment of spirituality and for the eventual realization, the direct experience, of God Himself. Of course, not many spiritual aspirants are able to engage in such practices for a large part of the day; it is given only to the very few to meditate long hours every day, or even to spend much time in external religious practices such as ritualistic worship. And how long do you think one can sing devotional songs? Even if a person feels inclined to sing all day, his neighbours will prevent him from doing so. The fact is, for the average aspirant no spiritual practice can be undertaken every day for hours at a time.

To speak of meditation properly so called — that is to say, sitting in a certain quiet posture, shutting off the outside world from invading the senses and the mind, and dwelling upon the Lord — we know that such meditation is impossible without concentration of the mind. Yet concentration is not easy to attain. Although we have been trained from early childhood to pay attention to what we do, this paying attention, which is nothing but the act of concentration, has not been well learnt by us. We find that our mind continually moves away from the thing or things to which we want to direct it. And when the objects to which the mind has to be directed are fine and subtle in character, as spiritual truths or realities are, such concentration becomes exceedingly difficult. But if we do not have concentration, even if we sit in the posture of meditation with closed eyes in a quiet place, apparently not paying attention to anything in the outside, our mind will be running races in many different directions. I admit that even such an attempt at meditation is of some benefit, but it will not take us very far. Year will follow year and we will find that we have not come any closer to God. I have seen such people. I have admiration for them. Even to be able to sit quietly without paying attention to any external things is a nice practice. But we want to attain *some* success in our spiritual endeavour; so we should not be satisfied with the external achievement of sitting quietly for hours. I sometimes am inclined to think that such a habit might even become harmful, an obstruction to spiritual growth. It is not meditation. As I said, without concentration meditation is not possible.

If you say that you will attain to concentration by a determined effort of will, I should warn you that while such determination may be fruitful for a time, sooner or later you will find that your nerves are suffering from the undue strain of forcing your mind to concentrate, and you will not be able to make any effort at concentration without bringing about some physical illness. This practice, therefore, has to be very carefully measured. How much should you concentrate? How long should you meditate? In these matters we ourselves are scarcely fit to judge. Until we have attained spiritual regeneration, we are greedy people – greedy physically, greedy mentally, and greedy spiritually. In other words, there is a vast impatience behind our activities; we want to finish everything quickly. Of course, we don't think we are impatient: we think we are just very eager. Well, when people express such 'eagerness' to me, I sometimes ask them what they will do after they have realized God. They have something else to do? You see, all you will do after having realized God is go on thinking about Him from eternity to eternity – there is nothing else to do. Then why this impatience? There is no necessity for it.

I understand that there is a loophole in that argument. You could counter it by saying, 'Do you suggest, then, that we should become lazy and not make a determined effort?' No, I don't suggest that.

I know that if you could take the view that henceforth all you have to do is devote yourself to God,
that in all the future you have nothing else to do, then
there would come a certain serenity of mind. Sri
Ramakrishna used to say that a crow once sat on the
mast of an ocean-going ship. The ship left port and
went far out to sea, but the crow was not aware of
this fact. When it noticed that the sun was about to
go down, it thought it must find a nice roost, and it
began to fly. But by that time the ship was so far
from shore that the crow couldn't find any land. It
had to come back to the mast. It rested a little, then
it went in another direction — again no land. After it
had flown in all directions and not found any land, it
came and sat on the mast quietly and calmly. Mind
reaches that condition; by and by a realization comes
to our hearts that there is nothing to gain in the
whole universe except God, and then impatience
goes away. I imagine that unless a little of that realization comes to our mind, we won't feel inclined
to take advice such as I have given — that is, to be
patient. But if this realization does not come to us
spontaneously, we have to bring it about by thinking,
by reasoning. Then our minds quiet down, and we
know our own measure — we know how much
meditation or concentration we really can practise
daily, or at any given time. But until we have gained
this inner sense ourselves, we should take the advice
of those who can give it to us.

Now, mind this, I am speaking of patience in

connection with people who want to undertake
spiritual practice, not with those who do not want to
practise anything at all. Such advice won't apply to the
latter, and I would recommend that they not pay
attention to what I have just said on this point. For
those who are reluctant to practise spirituality,
everything seems to conspire against such practice,
and a little determined effort on their part would
be desirable.

2

Well, as I said, most religions take the view that
meditation, prayer, worship, devotional singing, and
similar things are valid spiritual practices. There
have, however, been a few religious teachers who
have added more practices to these generally
recognized ones. I have specifically in mind in this
connection Sri Krishna and Swami Vivekananda, both
of whom taught *karma yoga* as equally valid. Everybody thinks, I know, that *karma yoga*, the path of
action, is not really a very high-class spiritual practice.
If I tell someone to practise *karma yoga*, he will think,
'The swami doesn't believe I can meditate; that is why
he is asking me to do that. I shall show him!' And he
shows me; *really* he shows me — but not in the way he
thought he would show me. You see, no one thinks
that *karma yoga* is really a spiritual practice.

Even our great Shankara in his commentary on
the *Bhagavad-Gītā*, which embodies the teachings of

Sri Krishna and is the first great book on *karma yoga*, has said that the practice of *karma yoga* succeeds only in purifying the mind, and then, when the mind is purified, other practices begin. In other words, Shankara reduced *karma yoga* to a subsidiary spiritual practice. The essential practices, according to him, are *upāsanā*, or mental worship, and contemplation and meditation. That is, only through *jñāna*, knowledge, which is derived through contemplation, is one able to realize God. That is his interpretation. Even those who have not taken such an extreme view of spiritual practice as Shankara and have not interpreted the *Gītā* as he did, feel that *karma*, or action, is not in itself a path to spiritual realization. For example, in contrast to Shankara, Ramanuja maintained that the path to God-realization is a mixture of *karma* and *jñāna*. He said it is *jñāna-karma-samuccaya*, 'the coordination of knowledge and action'. But here Ramanuja interpreted action in the very restricted sense of performing ritualistic practices such as external worship, and even before that, of doing one's duty according to the codes enunciated by the great sages. He did not mean any and every action as such; there was that restriction in his definition of *karma*.

As a matter of fact, you will find that even when teachers do not want to put forth their views in an extremely philosophical form, almost all of them will tell you, 'Yes, practise some action: do good deeds, worship the Lord, go on pilgrimages, serve holy people, do some noble work, and so on. Your mind will be purified and devotion will grow in your heart and through that eventually you will learn how to meditate, and in meditation you will be able to realize God.'

But suppose you do not care about God or about meditating on Him. Is there then any possibility of your attaining to the truth? If we read the *Gītā* itself, without being influenced by the interpretations of the commentators, we find it clearly stated that by the performance of action *alone* one is able to realize the highest. Sri Krishna says, 'By action alone Janaka and others attained to the truth, attained to Me.'[1] Of course the interpreters at once take hold of that and put a little pressure here and a little pressure there, and you find it is no longer what is stated in the *Gītā*.

I must say that after Sri Krishna, the one other great spiritual teacher who dwelt on this path was Swami Vivekananda. His book *Karma-Yoga* is well known. Don't seek in that book literary grace, or good organization of material, as if it were written for literary purposes. If you had heard the great teachers like Christ and Buddha, you probably would have found an infinite number of mistakes, grammatical and otherwise, in their speech. When these things were recorded by the disciples they edited them. Disciples become exceedingly sensitive to any imperfection in their teacher; so they begin to edit the teacher and the teacher's words, and by the time

[1]. *Bhagavad-Gītā*, 3. 20.

those words come down to you, you have nice little flowing sentences. The disciples have paid their debt to the teacher. But if you ever have an opportunity of coming across the literal words of a great teacher, you should never seek these things there — good grammar, good organization, and so on. Try to understand what they're saying to you; these are actually inspired words in a most literal sense. And Swami Vivekananda's *Karma-Yoga* is a book of that order. I have not the least doubt that as time passes it will become more and more a gospel of humanity. The Swami himself thought it was his greatest work. In that book he went so far as to say that one need not have any faith in God in order to realize the highest, and for his illustration of the ideal *karma yogin* he chose Lord Buddha — Buddha, who did not believe in God or any such thing at all. In other words, Swami Vivekananda pointed out that the practice of *karma yoga* does not require any kind of religious view, or, for that matter, any special mode of life or action. The fact is, a pure *karma yogin* might not be recognized as a *yogin* at all. He could sometimes be looked upon as one of millions — you would not see any difference in him. Sometimes, however, you will recognize this difference — he is not living for himself, he is living for others, living unselfishly. But sometimes you won't notice even this, because some *karma yogins* live solely within the scope of their normal duties — family duties, for example.

You have read of one such *yogin* in Swami

Vivekananda's story of the butcher, which originally occurs in a section of the *Mahābhārata* called 'Vyādha Gītā', that is to say, 'Song of the Butcher' — not that the butcher sang, but he gave instruction. You remember the story: a young brāhmin left home, lived in the woods, and became a great ascetic. By his austerities he gained some miraculous powers, and one morning he looked with annoyance at a crow and just by his look burnt it to ashes. He felt he had achieved, and so he returned to the world. That noon he appeared at the door of a house and expected to be welcomed, to be given dinner and so on. Nobody responded; so he became very annoyed. After a time the housewife appeared at the door. 'Sir,' she said, 'I am just now attending to my sick husband. After I have finished, I shall offer hospitality to you. No use looking at me like this. I am not a crow that you can burn me to ashes.' Of course the young man was flabbergasted. He had not spoken to anyone about what had happened in the woods. How could this woman know about it? So he waited, and afterwards the woman gave him dinner. Then he asked, 'How did you know I had burned a crow to ashes?' And she said, 'You see, I have a teacher. He is a butcher. And he taught me that if I did my duties without attachment in my heart, then I would attain to illumination. I do my duty as it is apportioned to me in my station in life; that is all the yoga I practise. But I do not crave for the results of it; I try to do my duty in the best spirit possible. And it is in this way that I have become illumined.' The young brāhmin became very eager to know more, and so she directed him to her teacher. She said, 'Go so many miles and you will come to a marketplace and there you will find him selling meat. Tell him that I have sent you to him.'

So he went to the marketplace and found a big fat butcher very busy cutting slices of meat and bargaining and selling and so on; he was covered with blood. (*Vyādha* literally means 'hunter', not 'butcher', but you see, in the olden days the person who sold meat had to go into the forests and hunt game and bring it back to sell. So butcher and hunter became identified.) Well, this butcher said to the young man, 'Please wait, let me finish.' Towards evening, when he had finished selling his meat, he took up his basket and said, 'Come', and he went home. Again he said, 'Please wait. I must attend to my old parents.' So he bathed and attended to his parents — bathed them, gave them dinner, made them comfortable in their bed, and after all that was done, he said, 'Now!' So the young man asked him a few spiritual questions and the butcher gave him a most inspiring teaching on *karma yoga*.

You see, there was no sign that this butcher was spiritual; yet he had become an illumined soul. Outwardly he was still killing animals and cutting up meat and selling it; further he was doing the duties which an average householder would do — taking care of his parents and so on. Would you call that spiritual practice? Most people have not called it so. Even if I were to become very eloquent and impress you with the idea that what he was doing was as good as meditation or worship or any other generally recognized spiritual practice, you might for a time be a little shaken. But the moment you got out of this hall, you would begin to say, 'Oh, yes, but the *real* practice is meditation. Oh, if I could just have concentration! *That's* the thing to do. How can I get concentration?'

Now, mind that, I am not against meditation and concentration. I am not saying that you should only work and not meditate. What I want is to speak to you of working in such a way that it will become as good as meditation, as effective and as productive as meditation. I am not against your doing other spiritual practices as well. But as I have already indicated, very few people are fit to spend their whole day in different spiritual practices one after the other. If one tries to do that, within a short time he will find that his body or his mind cannot contain the impact of it. Of course, one should do as much as he can; if he likes to meditate a little, morning and evening and so on, he should do it. If he likes to do ritualistic worship, he should do that; if he wants to sing devotional songs or pray to the Lord, he should do those things. Or if his teacher says that this or that practice is the thing for him, he should do it.

But still there will remain hours and hours of the

day in which one has nothing to do. Of course, if he or she is earning a living, or has to do many other kinds of duties at home or outside the home, the time is full. But then the problem would be how to transmute secular duties or activities into something spiritual. In your own life, if you calculate, you will find that you are dedicating only a fraction of the day to spirituality. The remainder is dedicated to worldliness, and how can you expect to gain in true spiritual knowledge if you dedicate only a portion of your day to it and the rest of the day to the world? You are a devotee of the world and you will continue as such.

3

There is a further consideration: We are living in a new age, and it has only just begun. This age will, I believe, continue for many, many centuries, and in the course of it a great deal will have to be done by man unto man. You see, this is the age of Man and not of God. Don't be frightened; the Hindu conception of mankind is not something divorced from God. But, if you are accustomed to thinking of man as separate and different from God, then I say the preoccupation of this age is Man — not God. I am not thinking here of the solitary few who always go counter to the currents of the times; no, I am saying that the major movement of the human mind in this age is towards the upliftment and glorification of mankind. That's the thing.

Swami Vivekananda, who was a man with authority to speak of such matters — he was the soul of this age — said again and again: 'This is the age of the worship of the *Virāṭ*, the visible God.' [2] Who is the visible God? *This* is the visible God, this which you see. The reality that you see, that which is real to you, *this* is God. This vast universe that you see spread before you, which you are perceiving every moment of your existence, *this* is God — boundless, boundless. This is called the *Virāṭ* in Sanskrit, which means the 'vast one'. 'Well,' you might say, 'shouting will not make it God; it is mostly just matter, with a little sprinkling of life and a little sprinkling of consciousness. How can you say that this is God?' I say this is God! Rub your eyes and see clearly! You are seeing things, as it were, with eyes closed in slumber. You are rarely able to open your eyes. Rub your eyes and try to open them; get your eyes accustomed to the light, and then you will find that what you thought to be the material world is not really material, but the actual Being of God present before you. And of this Being, Swami Vivekananda used to say men and women, human beings, are the highest expression.

Now, you should not confuse the Swami's concept of the worship of man with social service or with doing good to others. All those things are included in it; but it is something more. Swami Vivekananda never forgot that man is continually reaching towards divinity. Whatever a human being is doing here, even stealing, even murdering, he is actually reaching towards God. He wrote in one of his Bengali poems that when the thief steals or the murderer kills he is really reaching towards God in love, though he does not know it. Of course we say, 'Well, that's going a bit too far'. But then we don't know much. It is only an expert who knows. In medical matters you will admit your ignorance and will accept a doctor's word. But when it comes to studying the human mind and the movements of the human soul, we think we know everything, we don't need an expert. Experts, however, see rightly: they see that all beings are furiously moving towards the realization of their own divinity—that is all they are doing. Swami Vivekananda never forgot that. Never did he tell anyone that the only thing to do is social service. He never said that. Of course, you will find many Indian writers praising Swami Vivekananda, or his monastic order, for having instituted social service in India. Those who say that they don't know much. One cannot know a soul such as Vivekananda until one has given years and years of deep, meditative thought. Do you think you can grasp the movements of the mind of a Christ or a Buddha or a Vivekananda with just a little irritation of your brain cells? You should never think you can. Don't cheapen anything, because that is self-degradation.

One thing in the present age which I find most tragic is that human beings have forgotten their ability to be great. They have brought everything down to the level of a common mind. It is said the common mind is one per cent intelligent, and everything is being studied and interpreted with this one per cent of intelligence. That is condemning the human soul. Man has proved his greatness in past ages, if not also in the present age. But all these evidences of the greatness of the human being and of his profound depths are just brushed aside, and human history has been reduced to a recital of meagre achievements. No wonder, therefore, that there are millions and millions of average men who are becoming more and more dull. Very soon they will not have any brain left. No! We are great. Every single one of us is destined to realize the highest truth. Everything that we do is a movement towards that realization. In the *Bhagavad-Gītā* Sri Krishna said: *mama vartmā-nuvartante manuṣyāḥ pārtha sarvaśaḥ*[3] — 'Everything that man does in every way is really a movement towards Me, progress towards Me.' Swami Vivekananda recognized that same truth.

Now, you might say here, 'Well, if that is what we are really doing, then what is wrong with recognized spiritual practices? Let us forget man and everything else. Even to serve somebody with detachment means mingling with other people and

---

3. *Bhagavad-Gītā*, 4. 11.

living in the world—all these things are awfully upsetting. Let us get away from it all and go to a quiet place where nature is in harmony with our aspirations, meditate a little, and grow spiritual. What is the harm?' This is the harm: What view of yourself do you think you have when you propose yourself as a candidate for solitude? Are you not viewing yourself as a small, isolated being? And as long as you have that idea of yourself, how can you achieve much for yourself or for others?

Implied in Swami Vivekananda's teaching of *karma yoga* is a different view of God and man. As most of you know, in the summer of 1895 he and about twelve students spent six or seven weeks in a place called Thousand Island Park on an island in the Saint Lawrence River. And there he used to give most inspiring talks; it was a beautiful time. Some of those talks were recorded in longhand by one of the students and were published under the title *Inspired Talks*. When I was in high school I became very much enamoured of that book; I cannot tell you the delight I derived from it. It is so terse and condensed that every sentence provides immense scope for thinking and contemplation; there is no end to the depth of those sentences. And in that book there is the sentence 'Do not seek for Him, just see Him.' When I came upon that sentence it was as though a great light flashed before me. *Do not seek for Him, just see Him.* That's the essence of it. God is everywhere; what is the sense of seeking Him?

God is real. He is the only reality. He is *here* in this form. All that I have to do is to rub my eyes and see clearly. When we don't see clearly, then we see men and women; and when we do see clearly, we see God.

You will probably say that I am indulging in fantasy. No. I am telling you the truth, the literal truth. If you attain to that truth, you will find that all forms have become forms of God. Or sometimes forms just vanish away; all that remains is infinite divine substance. Or sometimes, if you are so inclined, you will find all these infinite forms have blended into one divine form. What do you think the form of a Christ or of a Krishna is? As Swami Vivekananda said, 'This universe is the wreckage of the infinite on the shores of the finite.' This whole universe is like a jigsaw puzzle, and each form represents one of the fragments; so just as you can put the pieces of a puzzle together and get a complete picture, the mind sometimes sees that all these forms have blended together and have become one divine form — the form of a Vishnu, the form of a Krishna, the form of a Christ.

Well, you see, when Ṣwami Vivekananda said 'Do not seek for Him, just see Him', that struck me as the very essence of the truth. Why should I seek Him? If I find this world to be real, then it must be God. Of course, if I don't recognize it as real, if I don't perceive it at all, or find it shadowlike, then I shall seek for God. But if this world is real, then it must be God. Whatever is real is God; whatever is existent is divine. So it is not a matter of seeking Him, it is a question of just seeing Him clearly. This is the same thing as the Swami's teaching that this is the age of the worship of the *Virāṭ*, the visible God. And having said this, he wanted us to continually reach towards God. The finite vision of this world is nothing but a representation of our ignorance; it has no place anywhere. And so there is a continual urge in us to transcend this finitude, this ignorance that is obsessing us, until we come to the clear atmosphere of true vision. That human urge is one thing Swami Vivekananda never forgot. He never forgot, further, that man is vast, he is the infinite Being. Every person is such; therefore all are one. It is this view of man which is behind his doctrine that we should serve God in all these visible forms.

Now, great teachers do not always think things out with the brain, as we do. They are really the soul of humanity, not just a small fragment of it. They represent vast sections of mankind, not merely of the present age but also of future ages, even a little of the past. In themselves they represent the aspirations and the understanding of a vast number of men and women, millions and millions of human beings. When a world teacher says, 'I want food', it is as if millions of hungry people through centuries and centuries were crying out through his voice for food. It is enough that he has said 'I want food'; he does not have to think about it. He has spoken, and he is not just one person, he is a million human beings. Swami Vivekananda once said, 'I am *man* incarnate.'

He used to feel himself at one with man. And he felt that in this age millions and millions of men and women will be lifted to their native dignity. The masses have been trampled under. A handful of people have lived in comfort and in dignity in past ages, while millions have slaved for this handful. Now the time has come when these millions will have their day. Strength will come to them, confidence will come to them, a sense of freedom, a sense of self-respect will come to them. They will enjoy the things of this world, they will enjoy the things of the intellect, and they will reach towards the things of the Spirit. This is the age for these millions and millions of people.

The Swami did not want them to have only a higher standard of living — central heating, wonderful clothes, plenty of vitamins, a nice library to go to, nice recreation grounds, so that the more leisure they have the more worthless they become, because they have not learned the use of time — either they spend their leisure time indulging in hobbies or they spend it in acquisition. Such things may give them a little satisfaction but do not make them any better: they do not discover any profound truth thereby. The Swami didn't want that. Of course he wanted people to have a decent living, a decent house and some enjoyment. But he wanted them very soon to rise above that material level to the dignity of their own inner being, spiritual dignity. He wanted even the common man to rise to that dignity; he did not want anyone to stop half way. He wanted all men and women — in the East and in the West — to rise towards that. That was his aspiration. Therefore one of his great teachings was, 'Go from door to door, the door of the poor as well as the rich, of the young and the old, of the learned and the ignorant; and to everyone say, "You are infinite, you are eternal. In you is the infinite power. You are free. You are divine." ' He wanted us to teach this truth to everyone, to tell them all that they are divine. That is what he meant by worshipping man as God.

If you say, 'That is rather a high philosophy for the common people to understand', his answer was that man *is* divine and so when you call him God he responds. He does not have to go through learned tomes of philosophy to be convinced of his divinity. If he were not divine, all these learned tomes would only mislead him; but if he is divine, he doesn't have to be given any argument. He has only to be told the truth with a sincere voice — not from the lips alone, but from the heart. That is what is wanted. If I have not experienced that truth within myself, my voice would not carry conviction to anybody else. But if I have felt this truth of the eternity, the immortality, the vastness, the wonderfulness of my own being, if I have felt I am the fearless one, the free one and that whatever the external conditions might be, nothing in the entire universe, gods, or men or devils, would be ever able to affect me — if I have felt this truth, then my voice will have a ring which will awaken the echo of this same truth in the hearts of others. And Swami Vivekananda wanted us to go with that truth from door to door and tell it to everyone.

I have not the least doubt that if we had done that in India, India would have risen much earlier — strong with an unaccustomed strength. His message was not the message of non-violence, which is negative and confusing. His message was the message of strength. Unfortunately, we did not receive that message as we ought to have done when he gave it. By 'we' I mean the masses of the Hindus. We shall have to listen to that message again and recognize that it is the only thing. Only then will India stand upon her own feet, glorified with a glory yet undreamt of by mankind. Swami Vivekananda often used to say, 'I see three hundred years of India's future before my eyes.' And he also said, 'The glory of India that is yet to be is so great that nothing of her past glory can come near it. You cannot even imagine the glorious India that is ahead of you.'

But this future is based on strong men, strong with the strength of the Spirit. Not aggressive, brutal men, most of whom are strong because they have some weapon in their hands. Such are not strong people even if they have physical courage, for, after all, they have that courage only as long as they have a strong body. There is an other strength — the strength of the Spirit, and that is an innocent strength. However, let me say here parenthetically that even if you pursue physical strength with the idea that your true nature is divine, your strength rarely becomes brutalized. Well, that is another subject.

What Swami Vivekananda taught was the strength of the Spirit, and he envisioned the man of the future as spiritually strong with responsibilities to all men. Now, I do not want to be dogmatic, and so I say again that I do not mean that Swami Vivekananda did not endorse practices of meditation or worship or prayer or singing, as such. There is no contradiction between these practices and the worship of man as God. But the latter, which has not been generally recognized as a most excellent spiritual practice but which has, rather, been ignored by most people — that is the teaching he emphasized, and it is high time we recognized it.

4

Remember this, as we grow in our inner stature our responsibility does not lessen, it increases. Have you found any great soul who did not feel responsible for more things and more people than does a common, ignorant person? While we are bound by worldliness we feel that our responsibility is only to a few people who are related to us by certain worldly ties. But when we become strong with the strength of the Spirit, we feel responsible for all men. That's the difference. We are part of the One. Do you think you can escape it? You cannot escape it. Moreover, this is the age in which the majority of people will have to think of others.

If you take a common-sense view of the situation, can you escape the fact that you have to give a great deal of time and attention to other human beings? In one form or another, you will have to do it. Either you do it from the depth of your own spiritual consciousness, or you do it under the compulsion of law. Why will you have to do it? Your country is close-knit. You don't like your children to grow up feeling that they are not involved with their fellow beings. You have to instil into the minds of your children as they grow that they owe duties to their neighbours. You may call it 'neighbourliness', but the word *neighbour* is sometimes interpreted in such broad terms that it loses its specific meaning and comes to mean *all men*, if not also extraterrestrial beings, who are supposed to come and annoy us with their saucers and things like that. You see, that is where your neighbourliness has extended. Can you ever think of people in this age saying, 'Oh, forget the whole thing, just go and contemplate and meditate and don't bother about others'. To a few select individuals you might give this advice, but not to the generality of people.

No, in this age we shall have to do a lot of work. A *lot* of work! The question is, in what spirit are we going to do that work? And here comes Sri Krishna's teaching in the *Gītā*. It's a most profound teaching—*karma yoga*, the practice of detachment. And here also comes Swami Vivekananda's teaching of the worship of man as God: 'God Himself has appeared as man; kneel down before Him and offer Him worship.' Every *action*, therefore, will have to be conceived as a form of worship. And it is this teaching I am thinking of when I say, 'Meditate while you work'. Because, friends, if you really want to do anything in this spirit, then there has to be a continuous meditation on the truth of yourself and the truth of others. Only when I keep within myself a consciousness of my own true being — that I am not this body, not this mind, but the infinite, eternal Spirit — only then can I look upon you as Spirit. The moment I think of myself as a body, I think of you as a body. The moment I think of myself as a mind, I consider you as a mind, and then I say, 'Oh, what a dull person that is! Oh, what a clever person that is!' You see, that is how the mischief takes place. Don't you forget it. The form of the external world is a reflection of your own thought. As Swami Vivekananda said, 'The world is you yourself mirrored, your reflection in the mirror, that is all.' If you cry, the world cries; if you smile, the world smiles. If you are wicked the world will look wicked to you; if you are pure, the world is pure. That's all there is to it. I will not be able to recognize you as the Spirit and serve you as such if I do not maintain the consciousness that there is only Spirit. You are Spirit, I am Spirit; that consciousness should be continually present. That is what I mean by meditating while you work.

Some have said, 'It's all very well to say "I am Brahman, Spirit", but it is difficult to maintain this consciousness unless you have given hours and hours to real meditation on God.' Don't you ever believe those people. They have never tried it; therefore they say this. Don't you see that your thought has made you what you are? Say you have a sense of fear. Why are you afraid? 'Well, all my life I have been afraid. Even as a boy I had a sense of fear.' Change your thought. If you were taught as a boy not to be afraid, not to fear things, you would not suffer from fearfulness today. Look at people who are brought up with the thought that they are masters; they are masterly in the way they behave. Just thought does it. Do they have to be trained in meditation in order to feel these things? They don't. I sometimes look at pictures of lion cubs. Even as cubs, they have a certain fierceness about them. You can well see that if you monkey with a lion cub he can look you in the eye and say, 'Remember, I am a lion!' That's it! Be a lion cub. Roar!

You know the story of the lamb-lion, the lion cub who had been living amongst sheep. One day he was caught by a lion and taken to a pool. The lion showed him his reflection and said, 'Look at yourself. Look at my reflection. Are we not the same?' The cub had to admit it: he was the same. And then the lion put some red meat into his mouth, 'Now, eat this!' He ate it, and he licked his chops. 'How do you like it?' 'I like it.' 'Now roar!' So the cub roared, and he became a lion. Friends, learn to roar and you will become a lion. Talk, think, act like Spirit, and Spirit you will become, meditation or no meditation.

Spiritual teachers will tell you that if you want to succeed in meditation you must maintain the meditative spirit all day long. Who can worship God truly? He who is worshipping Him even outside the hours of his formal worship. His whole soul is always at the feet of the Lord in worshipfulness. Then when he sits before the altar and worships the Lord, that worship becomes real. If at other times he chases other things, and when the hour of worship comes he suddenly behaves like a good boy and rings the bell and burns incense, do you think there is much worship in him? We have to maintain these attitudes; then they become real.

It is not that a person works all the time. My motto is: when I open my eyes may I see God everywhere; when I close my eyes may I see God within Me. If you are not doing anything, close your eyes, let your mind at once go unto God. If you are talking to someone, let your words be addressed to God and not to man. Why do you think that when Swami Vivekananda spoke to anyone, even a casual word, he just changed that person's life? Once he was staying as the guest of someone in Bihar. One morning he had gone out for a walk and he met a boy who was also out for a walk. He looked at the boy's feet, and he found that he had not tied his shoelaces properly. And Swami Vivekananda knelt down and tied the laces for him, and he said, 'My boy, you must not be sloppy,' and he went on. The boy *never* forgot that incident; it changed his life. Just this one meeting, just this one. It is a universal testimony that anyone who approached Swami Vivekananda felt the very best within himself rising to the surface of his consciousness. He felt that he was also someone, that he had a mission in life, he could be great. Instinctively all used to feel that way in his presence. The very best they were capable of would rise vividly in their mind. Why do you think it was so? Because Swami Vivekananda saw the very highest in everyone. He saw Brahman in everyone.

If only in very small measure, we have to do the same. If he carried many suns in his hand, we should be able to carry at least a few candles, but light we must carry. We also must see as he saw, then everything will become transformed for us.

5

In my opinion, the practice of *karma yoga* is an extraordinary spiritual practice. Just consider it arithmetically: You meditate three hours of the day; maybe altogether you specifically practise four or five hours. At least twelve waking hours will remain for you. What will you do with them? For the most part you will be working, and if you practise *karma yoga* at that time, those hours will become hours of spiritual practice. You will feel yourself as this vast Being. One difference between the teaching of *karma yoga* as it is found in the *Gītā* and as it is found in Swami Vivekananda's *Karma-Yoga* and in other places where he taught this path is that the Swami always emphasized that a person should think of himself as the Spirit, Brahman. Of course, in the *Gītā*, also, that is implied. Before Sri Krishna gave his discourse on *karma yoga*, which begins with the third chapter, he gave a teaching in the second chapter on the true nature of the soul. You remember that most extraordinary teaching — how the soul cannot destroy and cannot be destroyed? Beautiful teachings are there about the indestructibility, immortality, and eternity of the soul. That is the background of the teaching of *karma yoga*. And Swami Vivekananda brought it forward and made it explicit. He wanted everyone to have this consciousness within him: What a wonderful existence is this in which I find myself as the most excellent being! Nothing to be egotistical about, because I also find everyone else is that most excellent being.

Sri Krishna said:

samam paśyan hi sarvatra samavasthitam īśvaram
na hinastyātmanātmānam tato yāti parām gatim[4]

'When one perceives the same God equally existing in every being then he does not hate himself by himself and he attains to the highest condition.' And again he said: *śuni caiva śvapāke ca paṇḍitāḥ*

_____
[4] Ibid., 13.28.

samadarśinah [5] — 'The wise are same-sighted; whether in a *pandit*, an untouchable, a dog, a cow, or any other thing they see the same Being everywhere.'

When you begin to think this way, you find your life has become meditative. Behind your thoughts and your actions, even your furious activity, there is a sense of calmness, a sense of serenity and depth, in which you truly exist. Just as the profound depths of a lake may remain absolutely calm when its surface is rippled, in the same way you will begin to discover in yourself a deep calm and serene Being, though on the surface there might be incessant activity. And then that activity becomes coloured by the consciousness of your own deep being, which you cannot distinguish from Divinity itself. When you have become even slightly conscious of this fact, you have become transformed. Then, whether you are sitting calmly or are furiously active, your mind is in the deeps. I think that is most wonderful. *Here* is my God. If you say, 'This God doesn't seem very exciting, all this activity and these crowds of people', ah, on the surface it is not exciting, but go a little deeper, and you will find it is God Himself, nothing but God Himself.

Swami Vivekananda left the Belur Monastery to revisit the West in 1899, and it was during that second visit that he wrote a deed of trust in which he handed over the monastic order and everything pertaining to it to another disciple of Sri Ramakrishna, Swami

---

[5.] Ibid., 5.18.

Brahmananda. So (although that trust deed was not legally executed until 1901), practically speaking, when he left the Belur Monastery to revisit England and America, he gave up his leadership of the Order. Now, seen against this fact, the little discourse that he gave to the members of the monastery on the eve of his departure becomes highly significant. The monks had given him a farewell address, and then he spoke to them. And this last message to them was: 'Remember, our ideal is *vairāgyam* and service.' *Vairagyam* means 'dispassion'—consciousness is no longer involved in the body and the mind or in sense objects. He said, 'Maintain that *vairāgyam*, and then pour your hearts into service to others.'[6] Others? God Himself! The visible God. Remember, practically speaking, that was the last message he gave as President of the Order to the assembled monks.

Often I have pondered upon this message; it contains all the scriptures and all the prophets: Have no attachment to sense objects, be conscious of the divine within and without, and pour out your heart in service. There cannot be any higher religion than that. There cannot be a quicker method of spiritual illumination than that. There cannot be any greater means of self-fulfilment and service to others than that. I think it is a more complete spiritual ideal than we have ever known before.

[6.] See *The Complete Works of Swami Vivekananda*, 3:446-48.

RITUALISM:
ITS PLACE IN SPIRITUAL LIFE

1

Ritualism is one of the three elements you will find in any religion if you analyse it objectively. One element is made up of myths, legends, traditions, stories of saints and sages, accounts of miracles and divine visions, and so on. Some of these are historically right and true, while others, we tend to think, are the outcome of imagination or probably a mixture of fact and fiction. But whatever their origin may be, they serve the purpose of upholding the good fruits that come from religious practice. The second element is made up of philosophy or theology. Whether a system has been fully worked out or is just nascent in the minds of its followers, every creed or cult has its own reason or justification for its existence and its teachings. The major religions have very well-developed systems of theology and philosophy. As a matter of fact, you will find a number of such systems in a single religion, according to the tendencies of its denominations.

The third element — ritualism — is the one I am concerned with here. It is made up of the practices of a religion, which may be either visible or invisible. The invisible practices are essentially mental — contemplation and meditation. Of course, even those who undertake mental practices at least have to assume a certain posture, and to that extent their practices are not altogether invisible. But by invisible I mean that there is no participation of the body or of any external thing. There are other practices in which external things have their part, and the performer of such practices goes through certain routines, and all this constitutes what you might call ritualism in the sense in which I am using the word.

Now, if you have thought about this subject, you will understand that ritualistic worship is necessarily performed in relation to God with form. But about this worship spiritual teachers in India have made several distinctions: They say you can undertake an external practice, that is, a ritual or a ceremonial worship, and then, as a step higher, you can perform the same thing mentally. Afterwards, there is a still higher mental practice called contemplative worship, which is to be distinguished, on the one hand, from mental repetition of an external ritual and, on the other, from pure contemplation or meditation.

It is found that those whose idea of God is formless, impersonal, generally undertake straight contemplation. I do not say that there cannot be a certain ritual in their practice also, maybe an internal ritual (or a better word would be procedure), but it is purely mental. Then there is an in-between conception of God in which one thinks He has no form but possesses attributes—not many, not too human or too personal, but enough to make it possible for the mind to grasp Him and therefore to dwell upon Him in contemplation; even here, many people practise contemplation alone, without any kind of ritual.

But if you think of God as a self-conscious Being related to other beings, related to the universe as its creator and ruler, I would call such a conception of God personal, whether or not you believe He has a form. Many think that when the word *personal* is used it means that God has a physical body, or anyhow a form. Not necessarily. The body is just incidental. If no light were here and we could not see one another, we would still be persons, would we not? I shall still be a person even if I cannot see my own form, and you will still be persons if I cannot see *your* forms. It is the self-awareness in any being which is the essence of his personality. It is because of this self-awareness that he can understand another self-aware being and can relate to him, respond to him, and therefore have dealings with him. In that sense we are persons. So when I use the term *person* in speaking of God, you should always understand that it need not mean God has form. But God must have attributes to be thought of as a person, and these attributes are such that He feels a relationship with the creation — in its particulars or as a whole — and with the infinite number of living, conscious beings.

God as person is related to individual beings as the Lord. It is He who rules over us, and when our religious consciousness grows within us, we recognize that we are dependent upon Him. We do not fight this dependence, because we find it is very intimate, like the dependence of children upon their parents. We do not consider it a bondage, or if a bondage, it is a bondage of love and therefore not really bondage, and we try to come closer and closer to Him. Out of that comes worship. If you love someone, you want to worship him — that is to say, out of your love and reverence you want to bring offerings to him. That is what worship is.

It is no use giving the term *worship* any kind of technical meaning, as some religions do. You can worship man; you can worship a saint; you can worship God — it is all the same. There is no end to the intensity of feeling you can have for someone. How much you will revere and love the object of your worship depends upon your own capacity. One person may worship at the altar of God and be completely cold in his heart; whereas another may worship his father or mother and feel infinite love and reverence. The difference lies in the quality of love and reverence and not in the object of worship. In India it is quite natural to believe that if one can worship another human being with great wealth of devotion and pure love, he can thereby attain to the highest. Even if he has never felt anything about God but feels for his father or mother or for somebody else this tremendous love, this pure love, that will itself open his eyes to the highest truth. That is our approach to worship.

But however that may be, when you conceive of God as personal, you naturally do not feel identified with Him, as one does in all impersonal conceptions of God. You cannot think God is impersonal and at the same time say, 'I am separate from Him.' You may *start* by saying so, because there is no rule against talking nonsensically, but when you begin to think things out, you will find that you have to end by saying that God, who is impersonal, is identical with your own being, which is also impersonal. When your concept is personal, however, you always like to maintain a certain separation between yourself and the object of your worship, even if the separation is as minimal as a distinction. Why is it so? Because otherwise you could not conceive of the wonderful attributes of God and enjoy them.

You may say, 'We love Him; it is not a question of enjoyment.' But you see, in your very love for God you have an appreciation of His wonderfulness. In the heart of that which we call reverence and love is a tremendous, endless appreciation. It may not be conscious; it may not be an analytical understanding, but it is mixed up with your reverence and love. If you say of someone, 'Yes, I know he is good for nothing, but still I love him very much', that won't do. You see, either you don't really think he is worthless, or you don't really love him; you probably have pity or sympathy for him, but nothing more. In true love there is great appreciation. And such appreciation of the marvellous nature of God is not possible unless there is a certain separation or distinction maintained between the soul and God. It is in this relationship that ritualistic practice, external practice, becomes possible.

2

Now, it has been found that in almost all religions the Personal God is the object of worship, and, as I have mentioned, some think He is formless but full of wonderful attributes; they speak about Him as if He were standing behind a screen. Just as an ordinary human being would do, He talks to you, He hates you or loves you, He guides you, He does all sorts of things, only He has no form of any kind. You wonder, then, how He speaks. In all Semitic religions, where God is believed to be formless, it is often said that He has spoken to his prophets. His voice has been heard. Well, now, wherefrom comes the voice of God? The Hindus have been very matter-of-fact about this sort of problem. They say, 'No use quibbling about it. To ascribe everything except form to the Personal God is just fanaticism. Those who deny He has a form think and talk about Him in all other respects as a human being, an exalted human being.

Why can He not have a form?'

It is not, of course, a matter of argument. The Hindus claim that actually God has many forms, and there have been advanced devotees who have seen these forms. I need only refer to the historical example of Sri Ramakrishna, who had experiences of the formless God and also saw God in many forms. If we are to accept his testimony, then we also have to accept the idea that God can have form. It was nothing original with him; he only confirmed what has been known through the ages in India.

In Sanskrit books pertaining to this subject there are verses called *dhyānam*, whose purpose is to describe the form of a particular deity to be worshipped. Many such forms have been described in great detail — what kind of complexion, what kind of hair and eyes, how tall, how short, and so on. Those who worship God in a particular aspect or form memorize these verses and repeat them mentally so that they can form a mental image to meditate upon. That is why these verses are called *dhyānam*. *Dhyānam* literally means 'meditation'. Shiva, for example, should be meditated upon as a mountain of silver; he is white, like silver. Such descriptions are very helpful, and they are not man-made; they are not merely left to the poet's imagination. No, they have to be very realistic, very factual, because, as I said, many devotees have actually seen those forms of God.

You can well understand that the moment you believe God has form you take a human attitude towards Him. So it came about that the worship of the Personal God consisted in entertaining Him as you would entertain someone for whom you have great love and also great reverence. Without reverence you would not have the element of holiness, which should always be present in any form of worship. It is not enough to say, 'Oh, I love God!' Unless you have the sense of holiness, your love will not be spiritual, because it is in holiness that we become aware of the transcendental being or reality of the object of our worship. Until that sense of holiness has come to us, our mind will remain on this very same level, and although it is good to go through the forms of ceremonial worship because everything has some effect, they will not lead you very far. But it is expected that as a result of your going through these forms a sense of holiness will grow, and out of that sense will come the sense of transcendence—you will forget your own body and ego, and your consciousness will be filled by the presence of the deity you are worshipping. And when that happens, then your spiritual life—spiritual practice properly so called—has begun. Henceforth, as that mood gets deeper and deeper, you make your spiritual progress.

So there must be that sense of holiness; only then can you worship God as though you were bringing offerings to a human being. Sometimes in an advanced state there is no knowing what you would do. A kind of madness seizes you, and there is no formality about your worship. In Hinduism we have well recognized that state, and when a person seems to be in it, he is observed, and if he is found to be genuine, then he is highly respected. People think a real miracle has taken place: a person has come very close to God in true devotion and love for Him. Before that state is reached, you do things as your heart craves, but there is a method about it. Generally it has been found that people want to offer flowers and fragrance and light and food — these are some of the ingredients you find in ritualistic worship. I may say that generally speaking, at least in Hindu ritualism (and in Jain and Buddhist ritualism too), this human approach — let me say anthropomorphic approach — to the object of worship is the heart of ritualistic practice.

3

But that is not all of ritualism. When I consider this subject of ritualistic practice, I find there are at least three kinds of ritualism, and I believe that these three elements exist more or less in every form of ritualistic worship. The first element I would call magical; the second is the anthropomorphic approach of which I have spoken; and the third is the symbolic approach.

By the magical element I mean that you expect some unaccountable result through certain practices. For example, in almost all religions there have been claims about the supernatural effect of certain words.

Maybe some prophet or saint or sage promulgated a prayer or a set of words, and it is considered not only sacred, but also secret. A teacher gives it to you in private, and if you repeat it, it is supposed to produce a certain result. That I would call magical. Similarly, other practices are considered magical. In India, for instance, we say that if at midnight of the new moon you sit in such and such a posture in such and such a place and worship in a certain way, then a wonderful result will follow. You might well ask, why that particular night? Of course, there are physical differences when the moon is full or when it is completely absent. But why should the moon exert a compulsion upon the Deity? Why does it produce a supernatural result? And why at midnight? Just say at a quiet hour — that's understandable. But midnight has some special significance about it according to the Hindus. Old religions are full of such practices, and to say that they are all superstition would, I think, be going too far. I myself sit on the fence about it. I would not say they are all nonsense, because I have seen such practices produce results. But to understand them scientifically — that is to say, to trace them from effect to cause — would require such a penetrating and analytic study (which I have not made) that I will not pronounce judgement upon them. Suffice it to say for our purpose that in the rituals of most religions there are such magical practices.

If you will excuse me for saying so, the Christian ritual, for example, has a large element of magic in it.

You have to say that the transformation of unleavened bread and wine into the flesh and blood of Christ is something magical. There is nothing rational or factual about it. Yet a Christian feels sanctified by having partaken of that bread, because he has an instinctive feeling that it is not just bread. He eats bread every day — and much better bread that he has to take in church — and yet he has this sense of upliftment there. You may say, 'It is the general attitude with which he goes to that service, then there is the ceremony and there are chants and music — all these have an effect.' But that is not enough to account for the devotee's feeling of upliftment; he believes that the bread has actually become the body of Christ. Here something magical is being accepted in Christianity, and I should say that that is a very important element, even the main element in the Christian ritual.

But in ritual there is also the human approach. The attitude of a devout Christian towards Christ, for example, is utterly human. Although Christ is the Son of God, he is also the Son of Man, and therefore a devotee can come to God through His Son, who is the God-man. It is essentially an anthropomorphic approach, just as is the Hindu worship of the Personal God.

The third element in ritualism is symbolic worship. Now, some of you might well say that the Christian Eucharist, which I have called magical, is also symbolic. You see, there is a form of meditation in which a person thinks he is gradually transformed into the very object on which he is meditating: his body has become the body of God, his mind has become the mind of God, his soul has become the soul of God, and if he is meditating on God with a certain form, then his form has become that form of God. I would not advise you to try this out for yourself. Many of you read books or come to lectures and pick up some hints and suggestions and think that is enough for undertaking spiritual practice. It is *not*. Sometimes great harm comes. You have to know the right practice for yourself, individually. However, there is this practice of self-identification with the object of meditation. Now, one could easily introduce this meaning into the Eucharist. One could say, 'Yes, the bread is just bread, but it is a symbol of the body of Christ, and by taking it I feel that my body has become Christ's body and my soul has become Christ's soul.' I do not know whether or not Christians do that, but it would be quite possible to use this piece of bread symbolically — as a symbol by which you feel yourself transformed.

Or this ceremony of Holy Communion might have a deeper meaning (and I know that meaning is inherent in Christianity): it is the enactment of a great sacrifice. Christ is the priest, Christ also, as a form of God, is the object of worship, and Christ himself is the victim being sacrificed to this God. That is another kind of trinity, in which the same being is the priest, the victim, and also the Deity to whom the sacrifice is offered – the purpose being to enact that great sacrifice which is another name for existence. Existence, if you understand it, is nothing but the drama of sacrifice.

This idea that God sacrifices Himself unto Himself is continually mentioned in our ancient books, the Vedas and the Upanishads. We have a Vedic ritual called *Puruṣa Yajña*, or 'Sacrifice of the *Puruṣa*', which is actually the sacrifice of God unto Himself. I won't go into the details here; it is a fascinating idea, but I admit not an easy one to understand, nor is it the ordinary human approach to God. It is a very special approach that seems to have been in existence more in ancient times than in the present. Today, we want to love God – that's the whole idea – and although sacrifice is inherent in love, for us the sacrifice question does not really arise. In olden times in India every worship was a sacrifice. You will find the *Gītā* is full of that. But later, and even at the time of the *Gītā*, the motif of love and devotion began to assume predominance in the Hindu religion. I might say that in Christianity, also, although the priest goes through that ceremony, which is symbolic of a cosmic sacrifice, the general approach is that of love and devotion.

There have, however, been purely symbolic religions. For example, the Hindus' daily worship – the Gāyatrī worship – is purely symbolic. It is the worship of the sun as the symbol of Brahman. If you are a high-caste Hindu, say a brāhmin, and have been initiated into this practice, then every day you should worship the sun four times — at dawn, at noon, in the evening, and at midnight. That's quite an undertaking! So what many Brāhmins do they perform all four worships in one sitting in the morning; or maybe they will do two worships in the morning for dawn and noon, and two in the evening for evening and midnight. After all, they are busy people; they have to work their living, too. Yet they want to be faithful to their religion, and it is to their credit that, even though they practise in such a compromised fashion, still they do it, and they get their result. However, here I am concerned with this kind of worship as a symbolic ritual.

There have been many such rituals. For example, the old Vedic fire sacrifice, which is still done in a somewhat truncated form, is a symbolic worship. The worshipper lights a fire, as probably some of you have observed. He then gives this fire the name of the god to be worshipped, and makes offerings to that god by putting them into the fire. Similarly, sky, water, space, air, and mind are taken as symbols of Brahman. You see, in symbolic worship people start with concrete objects; then they go to objects which are still external but less concrete. Space is not so concrete as the sun or as fire; it requires a little more imagination to grasp space as a symbol of worship. Afterwards they go further and take the mind as the symbol of *prāna*, the life energy.

Now, what is the difference between an image

and a symbol? In the anthropomorphic or human approach to the Deity those who think God has a form make images of Him. When they install the image on the altar and invoke the presence of the Deity there, they are saying, 'Here He is — *really* He is here'. Then they go on worshipping: 'O Lord, please accept this fragrance; please accept this flower; accept this light; accept this incense; accept this food; accept my devotion; accept me.' That image is a symbol, but it is a symbol in the sense that a photograph is a symbol of a person; it is not just an indication or a sign, like *x* in algebra; rather, it shows what the person actually looks like.

In a true symbol, on the other hand, you find that one aspect of it blends into a certain aspect of the Divine. Take the sun for example. It has many aspects, but in my worship I shall dwell on its light, its tremendous light. You see, God has been called light, and in this respect the two are identical. As I dwell on the luminous nature of the sun, I think I am really meditating on the nature of the Lord. My mind dwells on the luminosity of the sun, but by some mysterious transfer of similar ideas, this luminosity that was always associated with a material orb in the sky becomes associated with my idea of God. Afterwards when I see the sun I don't think of it as a material thing; I feel it is the Lord Himself.

Now, if you say, 'Of course, one can indulge in all kinds of imagination. It is only self-deception; it doesn't mean anything', I say it does mean something, because the consciousness of God rises within you. Say you meditate on the infinity of space; although space is a dead thing, or anyhow an abstraction, by dwelling on its infinity the sense of infinity becomes transferred to the divine Being; so by your contemplation of infinite space as a symbol, you gradually awaken within yourself the consciousness of the being of God, which is also infinite. That is a symbolic worship. We feel that every ritual, to reach its highest effectiveness, should at least end in being a symbolic worship.

Sometimes one can *start* with symbolism, as in the worship of Vishnu. You may have seen sculptures or read descriptions of the image of Vishnu — a human form with four arms. But in most of the homes and chapels where Vishnu is worshipped, you find no human image at all. You see only a round black stone. It is a large pebble found in the bed of a certain river in India. People gather these stones, and when some one goes on pilgrimage he will bring some home to give to his friends for worship. Now, why is a stone worshipped? You all know that a round object is a symbol of infinity. But a truer reason is found in a description of Brahman in the 'Hymn to the Guru', in which it is said: 'Salutation to that guru who has shown me this Being by whom the whole universe is pervaded, who is *akhaṇḍa maṇḍalākāram,*' that is, 'of the form of an undivided globe'.[1] You might

---

[1] *Viśvasāra-Tantra,* 'Hymn to the Guru', 2.

wonder about that: You can understand that the infinite God pervades everything, but why should He have a spherical form? I know of one person who actually had that experience. He told me that he reached a condition where he saw God rising out of this whole universe in the form of a globe, as you might see the sun emerging from the ocean. When he told me that, I knew he had described the experience of the globelike form of God mentioned in this hymn. It is no doubt in relation to such experiences in which people have perceived God as the sun in the centre of the universe — actually living, not merely symbolic — that Vishnu, who is the Lord, was originally identified with the sun and worshipped as the Sun God and that the brāhmins thought of installing a round stone to be worshipped as His symbol. Many such symbols are really the result of experience.

4

In a true ritualistic worship the anthropomorphic or human element and the symbolic form of approach are well blended. Why? Because there is a danger in the mere human approach to the object of worship. If our love has become somewhat released from the limitations of human nature, human appetites, and human passions, then the human approach is all right, because it will bring the sense of transcendence out of which, as I have said, the sense of holiness grows. But if we have not reached this transcendence of our human nature, then whenever we think of love, even in relation to God, it becomes too, too human. It is not pure enough.

Well, devotees are rarely taught to direct human love towards God except in certain cults. For example, in Hinduism we have the cult of Radha and Krishna. Krishna is worshipped with the same love a human being feels for his beloved. But Hinduism also teaches that such worship should be undertaken only by very pure-hearted devotees; it is not for ordinary people. Chaitanya, who revived that worship and taught it, also had a parallel teaching. The religion he gave to the majority of devotees was that of singing the name of God, repetition of the name of God, formal worship with great ceremony, reading the holy scriptures, doing good to others. The higher form of worship—worshipping the Lord as one's beloved, with the same human love—he prescribed only for those who had become so pure that they did not remember whether they had a male body or a female body; they had lost all consciousness of their body.

But you know, some think that conditions like these are made by finicky people; one doesn't have to observe them too much. I have noticed a carelessness in this respect. People make light of the preliminary conditions; all they want are the high practices and the results they have heard about. After some time they will say, 'Why is it that I don't get any results?'

They have paid no attention to the conditions. Yet these great teachers laid down these conditions in all seriousness, and meant them *literally*.

In every religion there has been such abuse. Look at Christianity: every Christian who goes to church, eats a piece of bread, and does a little good deed thinks that after he dies he will have a place reserved for him in a very nice sphere. Christ didn't teach any such foolishness. Yes, he said that if people would take refuge in him they would have salvation. But taking refuge in Christ is no joke. If it were so easy, why are the major parts of the Gospels concerned with Christ's moral and spiritual teachings? These are scattered all over the New Testament: one should be pure, one should give up everything and follow the Lord, and so on. And these teachings —take refuge in the Lord or 'Here is my flesh; eat this. Here is my blood; drink this,' —occupy just a small portion of the four Gospels.

You find the same thing in India in relation to the *Bhagavad-Gītā*. In the eighteenth and last chapter, as you remember, the Lord said to Arjuna, 'You are dear to me. Give up all religion and ir-religion and take refuge in Me alone. I will save you from all sin.' Some people in India say that is the major teaching of the *Gītā*. They make a ceremony of it. When boys and girls reach a certain age, they put a mark on their body and say, 'I take refuge in the Lord. Henceforth I am in His hands. Everything is finished.' If that were so, then what was the Lord saying in the other seventeen chapters of the *Gītā*? Was He just talking nonsense? Well, that is *our* nonsense: we human beings ignore the hard part; we always go for the easy way. We don't want to tend the orchard or the garden, but we want the finest fruits and flowers on our table. We don't want to fulfil the conditions, but we want the highest results in our spiritual life. People have always had this tendency in religion. Therefore Chaitanya told the majority: go through a routine of worship so as to get over your weaknesses. Then, when you undertake higher practices you will get results — you will be able to love God truly. You yourself will have become the embodiment of purity and holiness; the love you want to direct towards God will have undergone a transformation. It will not be crassly human any more.

I was telling you that in ritual a combination of the human approach and the symbolic approach is absolutely necessary. And this is what I should like to point out: Ordinarily we think we are limited individuals, particulars, and the image or the symbol that we worship is also a particular, a small thing. You may meditate on the sun, but when you make an image of the sun in your mind, it is just a small sphere, not this big sun. Your mind cannot even conceive that bigness. So there is a problem. How are we to pass from smallness and limitation to the unlimited and the vast? How are we to cross the barrier?

Some of you will say, 'Maybe without worshipping an image anthropomorphically but by worshipping a symbol, we have a better chance.' Yes, those who by temperament have a more or less philosophical attitude towards God generally think He is without form. Although they may consider Him as a Person endowed with attributes, their tendency is to think of Him as all-pervasive, infinite. To them it seems too human to say, 'Oh, He is so kind, He is so compassionate! He is my Father, my Mother'; generally they prefer symbolic worship, because it makes them feel closer to their philosophical conception of God. But unless they have crossed that barrier, to them, also, symbols will remain dry and concrete and will not disclose this ineffable Being. They, too, have to become transformed before they can feel God as God and not merely as an echo of their own human personality.

So how is this to be done? You cannot do it consciously, although conscious efforts have to be made through your worship, your meditation, your philosophical reasoning, or the upliftment of your emotion. But I should say that whatever practice you follow — whether your approach is essentially human or essentially philosophical, it doesn't matter — it is only when you have transcended the limitations of human nature that the transformation is brought about. By 'limitations' I mean the smallnesses of human nature. Human nature itself is, of course, a limitation, but I am not speaking of that. I am speaking of the many smallnesses we have within ourselves *as* human beings — our attachment to sense objects and sense pleasures, and so on. When we have transcended these limitations, everything assumes a symbolic significance for us.

You have noted that one of the tricks of writing poetry is to find similes and metaphors. Why is that? It is not so obvious as you may think. The fact is, you see, the whole universe is symbolic. According to our own disposition, we have read meanings into things. You may say, 'Oh, we don't read meanings; we just see things.' That is what *you* think! When you have become accustomed to one meaning, it seems natural, and you are not aware that in the beginning you read that meaning into the object. The whole universe, everything in it, is unnamable, immeasurable, inexpressable. Its significance is indeterminate, but we, according to our state of being, read significance into it. When we are earthbound, or sense bound, we read a concrete meaning, but even then everything reminds us of something else, because the fact is that any one thing here is related to every other thing. In other words, everything is symbolic. When you have risen above your senses, you do not have to be told that everything should be studied symbolically; you will feel it. You look at the sun, at once you will be reminded of the infinite God who is all light, from whom all things have come. You look at the ocean, you are reminded of something; at a flower, of something else.

Well, to make this story short, Hindus have found that the things we offer to God in our human approach — flowers, water, food, incense, light — are the five cosmic or basic manifestations of God and can be offered as such. These principles, according to the cosmology of Indian systems of philosophy, are earth, water, fire, air, and ether; each has its distinguishing quality and is represented by a symbolic offering. A flower represents earth, together with the quality of odour, because the earth principle alone has smell. If you say water or air sometimes smells, they will say no, that is because some earthly particles are in the water or air. Well, you will find what stands for what in the ritualistic books of the Hindus.

But what I should add here is that if your mind has learned to dwell above the realm of the body so that you are not much conscious of it (I do not say absolutely unconscious of it, but that it no longer has any hold upon you), then when you offer a flower, thinking this is the earth principle, you will actually *feel* as if all that is of the earth, earthy, is given back to God. Similarly, when you offer the other principles you will feel they have been returned to God. And at the end of the worship, you will feel that all the elements of which the universe is made have become absorbed in God, and God and you are alone together. You will feel a sense of deep at-onement with God — in the silence of your soul, deep at-onement.

This particular worship, called *Āratrikā*, is done in the evening. The worshipper generally offers the five elements while standing and ringing a bell. The bell produces the continuous sound of Om, which is a nice accompaniment because your mind becomes concentrated and taken up by it. First, while ringing the bell with one hand, he waves a flower before the Deity with the other, offering it as the earth principle. Then he will offer water as the water principle. Next he lights a piece of camphor or a candle and waves it, offering the fire principle. He waves a fan to represent the air principle. Finally, he offers a piece of cloth, which stands for ether, the space principle, because, like space, cloth covers everything. If he has worshipped in the right way, this symbolic worship rings true, and as a result he finds all these manifestations have been accepted by God and absorbed into Him. One after the other, the barriers of creation have gone away; only God and the soul remain. The worshipper has lost outward consciousness, just as in deep meditation. *That* is the deeper and truer ceremonial worship.

5

Now, I have given a very cursory idea of what ritualism stands for. Let me summarize before I come to my final conclusions. First I should say this about ritualistic practice: If you are not capable of doing real meditation, then it is better that you do some ritualistic worship. What form that ritual will take depends upon your own nature. If you are of a very devotional nature and very human in your approach towards God, naturally you would like to offer flowers and incense; you would like to decorate the altar and garland the object of your worship. You could go in for all kinds of colours and all kinds of fragrance. It is very satisfying, very satisfying. I myself once practised ritualistic worship for a long time, and I found my nature congenial to it. I appreciate it, and I may tell you I have experienced its miraculous nature and can bear testimony to the fact that it is not just mummery and outward ceremonial. Nor is it paganism. The Western mind is full of such misapprehensions. What are you doing in order to feel close to God? Time is the measure; time is mind. I ask someone how much time he gives to religion. He tells me: 'Oh, on the way to the office, I think about it.' Fifteen minutes on the bus! You think that is spiritual life! If he had told me for fifteen hours every day he keeps his heart in God, I would say, 'Ah! *Something* there!' But we cannot do it. Let us accept that fact, we are not able; so we have to start doing what we *can* do. Otherwise we will never make any progress.

So this anthropomorphic form of ritualism is very good. Love Him — and with your love, there must be reverence. That is why you find so much ceremonial purity is observed in all places of worship. Those rules make you learn the art of holiness. How otherwise would you have a sense of holiness and sanctity? A housewife, if she is a true wife, keeps a chair near the hearth for her husband; she will keep his slippers there. When the husband comes, he will sit there. She will not allow anyone else to sit in that chair. She has built up a sense of sanctity about it. Reverence for God you have to have. Suppose you bring flowers for offering; you smell them, and then offer them at the altar. What kind of reverence is that? Reverence is an art in itself, and when you have learned it you will find that you have developed a sense of holiness and sanctity for the object of your worship. After that, long, long after that, will come intense love, and when it comes, you won't have to observe all these rules consciously. But that is another state. When Sri Ramakrishna was in that state, he would begin to eat the fruits and sweets that had been prepared for offering before the altar. At such times, the whole temple would just throb with the presence of Divinity, so that nobody had any doubt that some wonderful divine drama was being enacted. Nobody had any doubt.

So this is the way we start—with an anthropomorphic form of ritual. If you can do more, if you are capable of meditating, then add meditation to it; you will find it will be much more satisfying. Any ritualistic worship in which there is too much outward activity cannot go very deep. Therefore, the Hindus have said there should be lots of meditation interspersing the performance of ritual. At the beginning of your worship you meditate a long time, and then from time to time during the performance of ritual, you meditate. Of course, how much depends upon your ability and your time, but the general advice is that you should meditate enough to bring your worship to a deeper level, so that it does not remain too much on the surface. After a while you will find that ritualism has taken a minor part, and meditation has become the major part of your spiritual practices. And then later you will like to worship symbolically; it will come naturally to you.

Other practices can also be added to your worship. One is the repetition of the *mantra* or a name of God. In fact, that can be a complete and a total spiritual practice in itself. It is called *japa*. You don't have to do anything else; you just devoutly repeat the name of God. In order to do it properly, you should sit in meditation posture silently and calmly with closed eyes. But you can practise *japa* also at other times; when you are walking or listening to a conversation that is not important, or doing work that does not call for full attention, you mentally repeat the *mantra*. In this way, you can repeat the name of God for hours and hours every day, and that becomes a wonderful practice that can lead to the highest spiritual experience. Another practice which is very widely undertaken is singing devotional songs.

As a matter of fact, one estimate made of the different spiritual practices was put in this verse: *uttamo brahma sadbhāvo dhyāna bhāvastu madhya-*

maḥ.[2] *Brahma sadbhāva* — at-onement with Brahman. That has been considered to be worship, and that is the highest, the best. The middle state of worship is *dhyāna bhāva*, the meditative state. You have plunged into meditation; that's the middle form of worship. And the lowest form is the practice of *japa* and the singing of devotional songs and hymns. External worship, by which is generally meant ritualistic worship, has been called the lowest of the low. But here I should say in commentary that if, according to one's ability, ritual is interspersed with symbolic worship, which is mental, and also with long meditation, then it is not just external worship and should not be called lowest of the low. You have to give it a higher status.

6

In conclusion I shall say this: those of you who have been brought up in Semitic traditions are not much accustomed to ritualistic worship. You are accustomed to some forms of ritual, it is true, but ritualistic worship that is to be performed every day by the devotee himself is somewhat alien to you, and I may say that many of you would not take to it. Further, such are the circumstances prevalent today, particularly in the Western world — and I would say everywhere in the world, including

2. *Mahānirvāṇa Tantra*, 14. 122.

India—that people have little time for setting up a chapel and doing worship. So generally speaking, not taking into consideration solitary individuals here and there who have got a great deal of leisure and the necessary temperament, I am inclined to say that another kind of ritual is called for.

Swami Vivekananda evidently was aware of this need. His mind was not only attuned to the time in which he was born, but extended over centuries and centuries yet to come. That was his manner of thinking, and I do not believe his thinking was just speculative. You might say he had an intuitive kind of thinking; just as by deep intuition we understand the heart of another person, he understood the heart of mankind. And he said that this age will be characterized by worship of the visible God. By 'visible God' he meant mankind as a representation of Divinity—mankind as a whole and as individuals. According to his philosophy, Advaita Vedanta, every conscious being is God Himself; it is not merely that God dwells in the heart of every person, but that God alone is, and each one of us *is* God. I may forget *myself*, but I may not forget *you* who are the embodiment of Brahman. I have to say you are God Himself in human form, the visible God.

What kind of worship shall we render unto Him, this visible God? That worship you are doing every day. That is the great worship that is going on all over this universe. That is the great sacrifice. Parents make that sacrifice for their children; children sacrifice themselves in their turn. A grand sacrifice — or, if you want to call it so, renunciation and service — is going on; this is the very thing you are doing. A person working in a factory, in an office, or in the kitchen, a person cleaning the street, or standing on the platform and teaching — that is the grand worship and sacrificial ritual that is going on. It is to be understood rightly. For instance, I am not speaking to men and women; I am making an offering unto the Lord Himself. If I am true to my philosophy, these words are the offerings I make unto the Lord who is present before me in so many different forms. If I think rightly, I am now immersed in the act of worship. Consider how much absorption and concentration there is in everything that we do in our daily life — in preparing a dinner, in cleaning the house, in working in the office, in going from place to place. Our whole heart and soul is there; deep meditation is there. This grand ceremony is going on, only we do not recognize it for what it is. That is our trouble. Nothing is wrong with this universe; it is always God Himself, manifesting Himself, serving Himself, sacrificing Himself to Himself.

If we make ourselves conscious of the fact that everything we do we are doing unto God, that it is a worship, an offering, a sacrifice, then *here* is the great ritual; nothing need be changed except our feeling about it. Though I admit that when you become conscious of that feeling, everything will be more perfectly done. There will be no carelessness, no neglect; nor shall we recriminate against our own God. We shall not revile Him and rebuke Him and find fault with Him and hate Him. Whatever His outer form, what does it matter? God comes in the form of a saint, in the form of a sinner, of the learned or of the ignorant, of the old and the young, of the healthy and the sick, of the good and the bad. What difference does it make what His form is, when we know He who dwells within that form is the perfect God?

If you say, 'Oh, I cannot think like that', so much the worse for you! Let me tell you that until we have learned to take the truth to be truth, there shall be no end to our suffering. There is no magic by which suffering can be avoided. So the truth has to be accepted. Don't be in any way affected by the outside. Go within, and know that before you is this living Being, God. *Then* you will have the ritual of the modern age. And this is the ritual Swami Vivekananda expected us to practise.

I had the good fortune of undertaking this ritual also, so that just as I could say the other ritual has miraculous results, I can say *this* ritual also is miraculous. I practised it, and when I used to serve human beings, I could not but feel that I was serving the Lord Himself. And I may add that once you have got the knack of it, that is to say, once you have trained your thought out of foolishness into the path of truth, you will find it is the easiest practice of all, and the deepest. Ordinarily we live so superficially — no peace there, no rest there. Knowledge of truth and ignorance get mixed up in our minds. But the moment you try to look at things rightly, you take your stand on solid ground; you will look at things from a profound depth where there is peace and light and joy, and everything becomes right and true.

I shall add only this: If you want to practise formal ritualism, then put heart into it, so that very soon you can go beyond it. But you will make much greater and much quicker progress if you practise the ritualism that Swami Vivekananda taught: the worship of the *Virāṭ*, the worship of the visible God, God who is present before us as mankind and as individual human beings.

WHEN THE HEART CRIES FOR GOD

1

You are all acquainted with the Hindu doctrine and, for that matter, the devotional doctrine of every religion that there are two different phases of devotion to God. One has been called *vaidhi bhakti*, or formal devotion, and the other has been called *prema bhakti* or *rāgānuga bhakti*, devotion proceeding from true love of God. You know how a mother longs for her child when the child is away. You do not have to tell her that it is her duty to long for the absent child; it is a spontaneous feeling. She cannot pay attention to anything else, or if she does other things, underlying all her activities there is this pervasive longing of the heart; all the time she thinks of the child. In the same way a state comes to a seeker of God, one who has not as yet realized Him, when his whole soul runs towards Him. Even if he does other things, behind all those activities there is only a fragment of his mind; the rest is continually reaching towards God, wanting to find Him, to embrace Him.

This is the second kind of devotion.

The first kind has been called formal devotion because unless certain forms are observed by the devotee, he finds that whatever love he might have felt for God evaporates, disappears from his heart. I should not, however, give you the idea that from beginning to end this kind of devotion is just a matter of form with no sincerity or feeling; there has to be feeling, real feeling, behind it. It is called 'formal' only as compared with the second kind of devotion, which is spontaneous.

When the heart cries for God it is assumed that we have already reached the second stage, or are very close to it. Sri Ramakrishna would oftentimes say that if your eyes become filled with tears whenever you hear or repeat the name of God, you will know that you have approached true devotion. That is a very simple test. Some of you might think that Indian people do not know how to control their feelings; therefore at the slightest provocation their face becomes red, their eyes become tearful, and you might say that such signs cannot be considered true criteria of devotion. Well, I must tell you here that while there are individual differences, everyone, whether of East or West, who has gone through the preliminary practice of devotion reaches a stage where so-called sentimentality or emotionalism is completely abolished from his heart. He becomes very, very deep. He becomes strong of heart. You should never make the mistake of thinking that only weak-minded, emotional, soft people take to devotion and the strong take to *jñāna*, or the path of reasoning. That is an altogether mistaken idea. A true devotee is a strong person. How do you think he dares to embrace the infinite God, if he is not lionhearted? He could not love God unless his heart was very big, very large. And you cannot be large-hearted if you are weak. The weak are small, small in every respect. They're easily frightened, they cannot conceive anything very big in their heart or in their mind. So it is not for the weak-minded that the practice of devotion is prescribed; the paths of both knowledge and devotion are prescribed for the strong, not for the small. *Nāyam ātmā balahīnena labhyaḥ*[1] – 'This Self cannot be attained by one who is devoid of strength.' 'This Self' means God. God cannot be attained by the weak. Those who seek God have to stand the test of every kind of temptation. The world is continually tempting the mind; it promises all these tinsel things – things with an attractive appearance but underneath, pure hell – that is what the world offers to the soul. And do you think a person would be able to withstand all these temptations unless he were strong? No, he would not. So don't be mistaken.

As I said, when one passes through the preliminary practice of devotion, which has been called formal devotion, all spurious sentimentality and emotionalism disappear. And then when such a person

---

[1] *Muṇḍaka Upaniṣad*, 3. 2. 4.

repeats the name of God, or thinks about Him and feels his heart filled with emotion which finds expression in glistening eyes, those tears are not signs of sentimentality as we know it, nor are they expressions of national or individual temperament; they are sure signs that there is true love in the heart of the person. Of course, there are some poker-faced people; you do not know what feeling there is in their heart or what thought is passing through their mind. They are made that way. But if the eyes of a person who has reached that second state do become tearful it is a very profound thing, a very deep thing. Don't think it is easy to shed tears in the name of God; it is not.

That's a most extraordinary state, the state in which one's heart begins to cry for God. If you protest that you are not a devotee and do not believe in crying for God, but in *knowing* Him, I would say you are totally ignorant when you talk like that. Read the lives of the saints and sages of any religion; see the tremendous longing in their hearts, whatever path they may have followed; then only can you understand what longing is. There cannot be any more profitable reading than that; it is much more profitable than even the study of philosophy or theology or religious teachings, because the lives of saints are demonstrations of the truths you read in those teachings. You may speak of life, but only when you see a living thing do you understand what life is, how it functions, what its expressions are. Similarly, you cannot understand spiritual truths until you have seen them embodied and demonstrated in the lives of spiritual men and women, in the lives of saints and sages.

We are always talking of big abstract things; we talk of God, infinity, eternity. ... and I think a little caution in the use of such words might be very helpful. What do we know of infinity? What do we know of eternity? We don't know anything; we just use some words and a kind of vague feeling arises in our mind. Words are useless in describing things which are beyond speech. To know what infinity is, you have to see a person who has experienced infinity and having experienced it has become absorbed in it. As Sri Ramakrishna used to say, once a salt doll wanted to measure the depth of the sea; so it began to walk into the waters of the sea, and very soon it melted into the water. Those who know the infinite very soon become one with it. *Brahma veda brahmaiva bhavati* [2] – 'He who knows Brahman becomes Brahman.' That is what we believe. So if you ever have the good fortune of coming in contact with a person who has experienced the infinite, then you will understand what is meant by infinity. You will know what the infinite is through the way such a person behaves, the way he thinks, feels, and reacts. Otherwise how would you know?

When a person realizes that state he does not

_____

[2] Ibid., 3. 2. 9.

give lectures as I am doing — except those who, like a Swami Vivekananda, are charged by God to come back for the benefit of others. Only a very few are commissioned by God. That is the traditional Indian belief. They are the Incarnations and the divinely ordained prophets. They come to this world; they are not caught in it. They see the light as well as the darkness; they are capable of seeing both, and they drag people out of darkness into the realm of light. But, generally speaking, unless one is commissioned by God, one progresses from silence to greater and deeper silence, until one enters into Silence with a capital S. And in that Silence one becomes completely lost. One does not necessarily come back.

Today we don't make the mistake of thinking, as did the orthodox Christians in the beginning of the modern age, that this earth is the centre of the universe, but we do practically the same thing: we think that this miserable life which we call our existence on earth is the centre and core of everything that is, and it is in terms of this existence that we measure everything. Therefore you don't like the idea of people becoming absorbed in that silent Being; you always want them to give lectures and organize societies and go on talking endlessly. Why do you think this existence should be the measure, when·you know it is the very embodiment of all kinds of imperfections? Let one person ask himself this question: Has he found anything perfect here? If anyone has found perfection, it is only when he has gone beyond this life into the Silence in the depth of his own heart. As long as one has not reached that state, everything here is imperfect. We are dwelling in the intense darkness of ignorance. It is in this that we pretend to know, pretend to see; whereas actually speaking we are peopling our own darkness with our fantastic dreams. How can this be the measure by which we judge the highest? We should never think like that. If you think that to become absorbed in God is to be selfish, then be selfish! By all means be selfish! You will be truly unselfish by being selfish in that way. As it is, you are cluttering your life with nonsense; and pretending to be unselfish, you are cluttering the lives of others with your own nonsense. No. That is not the way.

2

Fortunate indeed is he who feels in his heart the longing for God alone! Even the most ignorant person is unconsciously reaching towards this infinite and eternal Being. According to Vedanta, although man is overcome by ignorance and has forgotten his own true nature, he is still somewhat aware of his lost self. If a prince were to suffer from amnesia, you would still see a kind of natural dignity about him; although he would not know why he reacts in the way he does, he possesses an unconscious majesty. We also carry that unconscious majesty about us. We who are infinite and eternal by nature, we who are always one with God, have forgotten that truth . If we were asked if we are infinite, eternal, we would deny it, our actions themselves would apparently deny it. Nevertheless, in and through all these ignorances there is a continual assertion of our forgotten nature, our divine nature. It is in pursuit of our own divinity that we are doing the things we are doing here. When a mother embraces her child and seems to forget everything in her love for this child, she thinks she has found the all and the whole. When a maiden falls in love with a young man and thinks here is everything that is to be found, she is unconsciously affirming this most adorable Being — the Infinite and Eternal One. Of course we all know the sequel to this infatuation. Very soon she finds that's not it. So comes divorce, or she gets accustomed to a life with him. That's all. The ideal has not been realized, but the search was real.

So you see, we have been seeking the Beloved, the Infinite One who has been called the most beautiful — as a matter of fact, He is the only beauty there is. It is from Him that all these fragments of beauty have come; it is His light reflected on these fantasies and illusions that gives us the sense of the beautiful, of the real. He is the one beautiful, beloved thing we have been seeking. Through the finite we have been reaching towards this infinite. As the poet Tagore said, 'I have plunged into the world of forms in order to reach the Formless.' Yes, we all know the form changes; the form is not there, but we have been hoping that if we plunge into the form we shall be able to reach the Formless.

Well, you know we have been doing this for an untold number of births — if you believe in reincarnation. We have been seeking this *Sat-chit-ānanda*, this infinite Being, infinite Consciousness, and infinite Joy through the wrong method, that is to say, through finite forms. In the realm of time we have been seeking that which is eternal, but we have never found it. Always there has come disappointment. And not merely disappointment; there has also come untold suffering. Attachments have been formed, and when we have been separated from those people or things to which we have been attached, then we have suffered. We ourselves have been snatched away by death innumerable times from things we have found satisfactory — at least, temporarily satisfactory. All those sufferings have left their mark on our heart. And through them we have gradually reached towards the idea that what we have been seeking is not to be found in the way we have been seeking it or where we have been seeking it. Gradually, at first very faintly, like the first streak of light in the eastern sky, this idea grows. True religion comes to a person in whom it has become a little clearer, has become definite. Just as you are at first not sure whether you are seeing the light of dawn, then gradually become quite sure that it is not just an illusion of your mind — in the same way a definite feeling gradually comes into your heart that there is some other means of finding what you want. Strangely enough, you have never thought it could not be found.

You might say, 'Why, there are agnostics who do not believe there is any such thing as this infinite, eternal Being anywhere. They have no proof.' That's the intellectually agnostic person, not the agnostic of the heart. Swami Vivekananda rightly said he had not met a single agnostic. He said if a man were truly agnostic he couldn't live. Of course there are intellectual, materialistic agnostics; *we* are such people, most of us. We thrive on thinking; we don't want to tell ourselves we are utter fools; so we like to think, and we like to think that we think, and out of such thinkers come agnostics. But people do not live by thought alone, a person also lives by feeling, that amorphous something, and in relation to that there is no agnostic; we never doubt that we will find what we have been seeking.

Yes, there *is* a perfect Being, a perfect person — *Puruṣottama*. The *bhaktas*, the devotees, are very fond of using that term *Puruṣottama*, the Supreme Person. Why Supreme Person? Because we have been trying to realize this desire of our heart in a person, not in a thing or an abstraction, but in a living being. And so if you think of the culmination of your desire, then you would call this Being *Puruṣottama*, the Supreme Person. Only there is a little catch here: by the time you have reached the Supreme Person, your idea of *person* has undergone a complete sea change. There is no form, there is no body, there are not all these niceties that come out of the finitude of people—oh, yes, we delight in people's weaknesses, but those are no longer there. You will not know when you were deprived of all those peculiarities which make a person a person to you; they have just dropped off. You see, a person really is not what we think him to be. A person does not necessarily have a form, does not necessarily have any of these finite characteristics; a person essentially is a formless being, a perfect being, but he is self-conscious and capable of responding to every function of consciousness in another person. That is the essence of a person. And so when you have passed through these changes and have arrived at the Supreme Person, *Puruṣottama*, you have found the infinite Being whom you have been seeking through innumerable births and deaths, through endless experiments and testing. You have been going through all these experiences, and you have arrived at this perfect and supreme Being—and you have never had any doubt that He was there.

You have never had any doubt, but when the condition of which I was speaking has been reached conviction grows, and then, like the definite light of dawn, the certainty is in your heart that there *is* someone in whom all your dreams will be realized and that He is not in the things in which you have been seeking Him. Your heart becomes unified; all the desires of your heart become drowned in this one desire.

Some people will tell you, 'Don't go off the deep

end.' Hang on to poison—a cup of poison in one hand and a cup of nectar in the other. Drink a little sip from this and quaff from that. That is the advice given by fools, who, according to worldly people, are very wise. Worldly-wise people are greater fools than merely worldly people. They are representatives of Satan—really. They pretend to be wise, and therefore they have a hold over you, and they will keep you in the world by hook or by crook. Of course, if you are a worldly person and want worldly advice, go to them; who cares what you do or don't do in this world? But here we are concerned with spiritual knowledge, and if you want guidance in spiritual things, do not listen to such advice. Do you think drinking poison and nectar at the same time will make you immortal? No. You have to drink only nectar. You have to go all the way. And do you think you can go all the way if you are not ready for it? Many people think they have only to incline and they will roll over. Let me see how they roll over; they cannot. To reach that intense state of longing, you have to try and try and try; you have to cry your heart out, laying yourself prostrate at the feet of the Lord. It is not as easy as you think. You have to make a continual effort to unify your desires.

Multifarious desires have taken hold of our souls; there is no end to them. Yet, oddly enough, under the guise of these innumerable desires you are seeking only a few gross things. If you really analyse your desires and come to their common denominator, you will find them so gross, so beneath your human dignity that you will be ashamed of having them; you will be surprised. We have learned the great art of camouflage: we have the grossest desires, but we have put a most alluring appearance upon them, a most dignified appearance. Under this appearance of dignity there is a craving for the gross; if that were not there, we would at once become free, spiritual. So analyse your desires, and you will become ashamed. There is a practice in almost every religion — Buddha himself used to prescribe it very ardently: find fault with the objects of your desires; they *are* faulty. At first you will refuse to think them so; you see, glorifying them is the first thing we do.

Now, I am saying all these terrible things, and no doubt protests are rising from at least some hearts. You will say, 'The swami is too extreme; things are not that bad. I have met wonderful people.' Yes, of course, I also have met wonderful people. As a matter of fact I think everybody is wonderful. I can say all these terrible things from the platform, but when I come face to face with a person, I cannot say them. You see, I can be very impersonal from here, but when I meet a living person I cannot stop with his appearance. Even if he were to make a thousand mistakes, I would be bound to see something exquisite beyond those mistakes, and I couldn't take this hard attitude towards him. My opportunity of saying harsh things is the platform. Yes, everybody is wonderful, but that's not the point.

The point is that we, being wonderful, have been caught in this mess, and we want to get out of it. That's the problem. It is really the greatest tragedy that a wonderful being has been caught. If we were not wonderful, if we were really miserable creatures and a miserable state were really ours, then there would not be such a tragic sense. If a fool, a congenital fool, behaves like a fool, you are reconciled to it. But if you have known a very intelligent person and he or she suddenly becomes an idiot, your heart will be deeply saddened. Great persons we are, all of us! Yet we have been caught in the ignominy of this miserable finite life. That is the tragedy. Therefore we should see this life as Buddha and all great teachers have taught us to see it: it is not worth living; we should rise above it. If we see life in this way, we can get free of our desires to a great extent.

3

I shall come later to a further discussion of the ways and means by which this intensity of longing for God can be achieved, but let me here go on with a description of that state. It has been said in one of our holy books, the *Śrīmad Bhāgavatam*, that the lowest class of devotees are those who worship the Lord on an altar or in a symbol with great devotion; formal worship they do, but they have no particular attachment for the devotees of God, they are indifferent about them. The middle class are those who worship God and respect and appreciate every form of worship. They have great love for devotees; for good people who may not be devotees they have friendship; and towards those who are not good they are indifferent. The highest class of devotees are those who recognize God in any form; to everyone their love goes — good and bad, devotees and those who are not devotees; they feel the presence of God in everyone, and therefore they love everyone. As Sri Ramakrishna said so nicely and strangely, 'Well, am I suffering from jaundice?' You know when a person suffers from jaundice everything looks yellow to him; so he said, 'Am I suffering from jaundice? Wherever I look I see God.' Isn't it a wonderful way of saying such a tremendous thing?

Of the person who is first feeling this tremendous longing for God, we may say that he belongs to the middle group; he has not yet reached that state where he sees God everywhere; he still sees little distinctions. If he meets a great devotee, he becomes excited about him. He does not want him to leave. If the devotee goes away, his heart is broken. Tulasidas, a great saint, once said, 'Both these kinds of people cause me misery — the wicked by their wickedness and the saintly by their saintliness, because when I am separated from the saintly my heart breaks.' Yes, that is the way it is: he deeply loves the devotees. It is not a binding love, not the love of worldly people, but there is the same intensity of feeling. Towards all good people his friendship goes, and from those who are worldly, he shrinks away.

A very great poet, who was living a worldly life, once came to visit Sri Ramakrishna and asked him to please give him some advice. Sri Ramakrishna could not speak to him. Later he said, 'I tried hard to speak to him; a power seized my tongue, would not allow it to move.' To a small extent that is the kind of thing that instinctively comes to a devotee. This may not sound nice, but I am giving a description of that state, and this is a symptom. You can make of it what you want; you may like it, you may not like it, but that is what it is. There is no egotism nor hatred involved in it; it is just an instinctive reaction, without judgement. If you accuse such people of being critical of others, they would be horrified. The devotee is not aware of good or bad; he just bows at the feet of everyone. To him everyone is the child of God.

Physically, particularly as he progresses, such a person loses his appetite, that is to say, he loses his desire for material things like food and drink and sleep and other kinds of physical enjoyments. He becomes very casual about them. Some people are born that way. According to our understanding, we Hindus say that in their past incarnations they have achieved this state—they have gone through their period of struggle and have achieved this freedom from desire. When Sri Ramakrishna saw Swami Vivekananda for the first time he was very much impressed by him. He said, 'I found the boy had no consciousness of where he was or what he had on or where he sat.' He had no consciousness of those things at all. Just imagine the beauty of that state! How much of our energy and time and feelings are involved in little things — what food we eat, what kind of house we live in, what kind of clothes we put on, how we appear to others. Am I looking attractive and right, or are crow's-feet appearing and grey hairs coming? — all these big problems are on our heart. Our whole life goes like this; we have a keen sense of competition, expressed or unexpressed, and we are caught in those things. But these people get beyond all that. Further, they get beyond a sense of time. Night comes, day comes — they don't know any difference. We always associate night with sleep, and so we fall asleep at night. Not so with them; nor are they overcome by a sense of fatigue. A little rest and they are as fresh as ever.

It is said of the sleep of people in this middle state that they do not lose consciousness, they only lose consciousness of external things, and another kind of consciousness comes alive in them, which can be likened to meditative consciousness. They become unaware of the external: if someone speaks near them, they don't hear it; if somebody touches them, they don't feel it, and yet deep within there is a greater consciousness awakened. When one wakes from this kind of sleep he feels as if he has come out of a very deep meditation. Sleep for him therefore is superior to waking consciousness, because in waking consciousness he has to be aware of the world of relative forms, but when he is asleep he is free from this involvement in sense perception, and he becomes conscious only of that which is beyond the senses – of spiritual existence, God.

If you ask such a person what he wants, does he want name and fame, does he want anything of the senses? No. If you ask him, 'Sir, what shall I give you for your birthday?' it is hard for him to come to a conclusion about it. 'Can I get something for you?' It is not easy for him to say at once, 'Yes, I want this.' His mind has changed. If people honour him or dishonour him, all right. If the body is healthy or ill, all right. Not that he doesn't take care of his body; he will take reasonable care of it. But in spite of everything, illness does come to the body; if it comes, let it come.

Some of you think that if you are spiritual your health should bloom. I don't know what the body has to do with spirituality, but by all means let it bloom. I, too, want it to bloom, but let it do so without asking a price from spirituality. If it doesn't ask that price and it blooms, welcome. If it doesn't bloom, that also is welcome. If God can create health, you like it; if He creates illness, you don't like it. But whatever has been touched by His hand is celestial, wonderful! Don't ever mistake it. Life is wonderful, because He created it. *Death* is wonderful because He created it. Health is wonderful, illness is wonderful, because *both* have been created by Him. Or don't you think so? You think God created half of it and the other half was created by somebody else? Then that somebody is also a creator, equal to God. Of course, there are some who will not admit that; instead, they go through all kinds of gyrations of philosophy and reasoning to prove health is created by God but illness is not. Well, I confess I have not been able to grasp the essence of such arguments. Simple-minded as I am, I come to the conclusion that if anything is created by God, then *everything* is created by Him; so why hug good health and not ill health? As a matter of fact, let us forget all these things. From a psychological point of view, he alone conquers ill health who is not affected by it.

Conquest! That's the watchword of the strong. My friends, be victorious! Conquerors we are! We shall conquer life, we shall conquer death, we shall conquer health as well as illness. And you conquer these things not by fretting and fuming and running here and there, but by rising above them, by becoming indifferent to them. If you ask, 'Can we be indifferent to ill health?' of course you can be indifferent to ill health. Of course! If you are strong, you can. If you are weak, then you cannot conquer even health, what to speak of illness. Health will make you a pawn of its game. Health says, 'Food!' — go on stoking this body. Health says, 'Exercise!' — run, go to a gymnasium, do all these things. Health says, 'Sleep!' — ten o'clock, snoring. Health has made a victim of you. You think health has given you a gift? No. You are a dupe of health; don't you forget it. If you want spirituality, don't you forget it. Spirituality has nothing to do with health or illness. Both come because the body is made of a material that passes through these alternate states and eventually disintegrates — and that is called death.

Internally, what are such people seeking? Day and night they seek the Lord alone. They repeat His name, they look at His likeness. If a person is a devotee of Christ, he will look at his picture. The same symptoms appear in a human being who has fallen in love with another human being. He likes to have the beloved's photograph, he looks at it again and again — discovers one thousand and one beauties — he sees beauty in every feature; even ugliness has become exquisitely beautiful. Then he would like to draw his beloved's picture. Of course, only if you believe God has form, or if you are devoted to an Incarnation of God, can you paint His picture. But they say it is one of the signs of devotion and, therefore, one of the practices of devotion, a very effective practice. Just as composing devotional songs makes the mind dwell upon God, painting His picture also makes the mind dwell upon Him.

They sing unto Him, they dance unto Him, they want to have His image and decorate it. You may ask, 'What is the sense of decorating an image or a picture?' Well, you see, love is a sort of madness, isn't it? A mother will take the picture of her baby and will kiss that picture. What is there in kissing a piece of paper? Does the mother think like that? No. If she thought she was kissing a piece of paper she would become startled. She was thinking of kissing her baby. But one thing you must remember here, and that makes the difference: a mother may not admit she is kissing a piece of paper; yet she will admit it is not the baby she is kissing but a *picture* of the baby. But about God this need not be true. Why? Because, you see, the baby cannot come to the picture; the baby may be five miles away; he cannot enter into that picture. But when a devotee puts a garland around a picture or an image of God, He, being everywhere, has a tendency of entering into that image and taking that garland. He is a very greedy person, a very greedy person. He will come there so that He can enjoy that garland. You are singing before this image? He will come with all ears and sit in the image listening to your song. He doesn't want to miss anything. And how wonderful that is for us! The great teachers of devotion have always said that God, the object of love that He is, responds even to the slightest expression of love from anyone. You have to accept that as a fact. Just as the *jñānis*, the philosophers, say that everywhere, in everything, the supreme Being is equally existent, the *bhaktas*, the devotees, say that the object of their love is everywhere; where even the slightest devotion rises from the heart of the meanest of His creatures, He responds there equally.

So in various ways a devotee in the middle state wants to enjoy God. He wants to love Him. And then from time to time he will close his senses and in deep silence feel His presence and meditate upon Him.

Friends, in the path of devotion almost all the teachers have emphasized one aspect of divine existence, which is that God dwells in the heart of every being. That is one of the essential points in this path. And it has been found that a devotee likes very much to meditate upon God, to feel His presence in his own heart as the Soul of his soul. Where else would he feel Him, where else would he embrace Him? Tell me where. If you say, 'Why, outside', well, even when he sees God in the outside and embraces Him, the action takes place within himself, because there is no such thing as 'outside'. Everything is in consciousness, in the soul. If you say, 'The world is outside' — never believe that nonsense! The world is in consciousness. Where else would it be? When you say, 'I see a tree', all you are saying is, 'There is a tree in my consciousness'. Are you saying anything else? You become conscious of something only when it is in your own consciousness. There is no sense in saying, 'There is a tree outside my consciousness'. Much less would it be true to say 'God is outside my consciousness'. Devotee or *jñāni* — whatever you are — all that takes place is in your soul. Why do you think a person in love wants to embrace the object of his love? He wants to put the other person inside his soul. That is what he's trying to do; but he follows the wrong method. A mother clasps her baby to her heart; she feels deep in her heart a satisfaction. That is where the reaction takes place. The devotee wants to feel the presence of the Lord in his own heart; so from time to time he meditates upon Him as shining there in His blessed glory. If he finds that the Lord is not there, he will become frantic, as if his heart would break.

I sometimes quote from a poem by one of the great saints of India. He was also a great Sanskrit scholar, and his verses are so pregnant with meaning that they are looked upon as having the same authority as scripture. In one of his poems he described a state of devotion:

yugāyitam nimeṣeṇa cakṣuṣā prāvṛṣāyitam
śūnyāyitam jagatsarvam govindaviraheṇa me[3]

—'When I am separated from the Lord, one moment appears to me like an age, and my eyes begin to shed tears like a rain cloud heavily shedding rain, and the whole world seems empty, as if all substance has gone.' May I add further that when that state comes, even the brightest sun seems engulfed in darkness, all light vanishes from the face of the earth. That is the kind of grief that comes to the devotee's heart. Sometimes you will find he cries his heart out in agony. And then comes peace, and his face is filled with joy.

There is only one way to understand it: in terms of human love. Otherwise it will appear rather a strange state to go through. But you know, if we truly love, humanly speaking, all these symptoms come. The only difference is that in the realm of the senses and in terms of finitude the whole thing is doomed to

---

[3]. Sri Chaitanya, 'Eight Verses of Instruction', vs. 7.

eventual failure. Spiritual love takes you out of the realm of the senses, and instead of dooming you to failure will take you to success; you will be united with this object of your love from eternity to eternity. That's the difference, but the symptoms are the same.

Some of you may raise this question, 'What good will it do me?' What good does it do anyone to fall in love? Go and ask a lover; he will look upon you with pity in his eyes. Love is the fulfilment of life. Neither earning much wealth nor gaining great fame nor knowing many things fulfills a man, but he is fulfilled when he can feel at one with at least one other being. That is love. Isolation is death; union is life. That is why you find men are gregarious: everyone wants someone to love, if not another person, at least a canary or a dog. Something to love. It is a symbol of his unification with the other existence, represented not by himself but by the rest of this universe. That is the answer: love is the fulfilment of itself. It is its own end.

If you want to be philosophical, then I say that love is also the realization of truth. If I speak philosophical, logical language, you will at once accept it. If I say our true nature really is infinite; everything is infinite; therefore we should feel at one with everything, you will say, 'Yes, that's right, that's the truth.' But we can also speak the language of love. I have always thought that monism could be spoken of in either of these two ways: in the language of love as well as in that of logic — the language of the heart as well as that of the intellect. Although, generally speaking, logical language is used to express truth, I think one should make an effort to use the language of the heart to express the same truth, in order to eradicate this misconception about the quest for truth. And isn't it the same thing? The same psychological state applies to both ways.

If you follow the path of logic, your philosophy will tell you that if you want to find this one Being you must go beyond manifold existence, beyond the world of name and form, as they say. How do you do it? As long as you are interested in the world of name and form, this external world, you will never be able to go beyond it. Never! Neither in regard to yourself nor to others. If I am to perceive this formless, nameless Being which I truly am, this eternal, infinite Spirit which the human soul truly is—which I am, which you are—I have to go beyond the symbol of limitation, beyond my own form, which is the mind as well as the body, and also beyond the name, which is the idea in the mind. I have to go beyond both. As long as I seek the comforts of the body, as long as I crave the things which can be had only through the body, I am the prisoner of the body, I have become one with it; I cannot get beyond it. That is why all religions have said give up, give up, give up. Give up the things of the senses. As long as you are still attached to those things, you cannot find the truth. The moment you have given up your desires, you will become free from this body; it will appear separate from you. Just as this robe feels separate from me, although I know of its existence around my body, so your body will feel separate from you. Then you will begin to feel yourself as the Spirit. So in the primary stages of whatever path you follow you continually try to cut the bondages by which the soul has been tied to the body. And when we rise above name and form, we become aware of this one Existence.

What has happened? As I have already indicated, sense desires are false representations of the true desire for God, and when we discover this fact, our desires all become unified. All the emotions, all the forces of the mind just blend themselves into one, and this one becomes the longing for God. You see, when this tremendous longing was scattered in the form of many sense desires, our life was a poisonous swamp; but when we give those desires the right direction, then we find they all become joined together and become a mighty and powerful river, sweet, wholesome. That is exactly what happens to a person who has reached that state of longing: the search for beauty, for sweetness, for love and affection, for power and security, for the perpetuity of existence, for the sense of harmony with all, possession of all, unification of all — all our aspirations are blended into that one great longing. And we know that the fulfilment of that longing is He who is the source of everything we seek here — infinite love, infinite life, infinite power, infinite wisdom, infinite goodness, infinite peace, infinite harmony. Yes, He is the all.

Now, when one has reached this longing of the

heart, one cannot stop there. From our standpoint that might seem a wonderful achievement, but from the standpoint of the person who has reached that state, it is just the beginning of further effort. He or she wants to undertake all kinds of spiritual practices. If you have that longing, you can do a great deal; your body will accept it. Whether you eat or not, sleep or not, whether you are physically strong or weak, you can do a tremendous amount of spiritual practice. Before that, everything has to be regulated, everything has to be done according to form, but at that time you undertake unheard-of struggles. Why this struggle? Because although the gross form of disunion has been conquered in the mind, subtle forms are still there; they have not yet been conquered, and if one is incautious these subtle forms of division have a tendency to reappear. You sometimes hear of a very spiritual man suddenly turning worldly, and you wonder how it happened. Incautiousness probably has brought him down. It is these subtle desires that you are now conquering; you are trying to uproot everything. If you want to clear a plot of ground, you cut down the trees and also take out the main roots; yet perhaps some small roots have remained underground, and after a time sprouts come from them; these are the things you now want to root out for good. A person in that state is almost fearsome to an ordinary person. If you come near him, and if you have insight, you would be frightened by the tremendous intensity of his mind. You would not even understand him; such people are no longer like ordinary people, that you can judge them by your standards.

Well, as a result of that effort comes God-vision. The last traces of finitude disappear from the soul. Sometimes that state — the highest state of devotion — has been spoken of as the death of the mind. Mind is the symbol of finitude; Spirit is not. It is the Spirit that knows the Spirit; man the Spirit knows God the Spirit. That state is the worship of the Spirit by the Spirit, as Swami Vivekananda said. And, you see, that is the state indescribable. Of course, in one generation very few reach it, and rarely do we know them. Some of you might think that if a person has become a saint we would know about it. No. It is said in our books that sometimes they appear like fools or like dunces. How shall we know who has reached that state? Only a knower of God would be able to recognize such people. Some, of course, we do know, because, as I said earlier, they assume a mission among men; otherwise we are not apt to know of them. But in any case you should remember always that that state is not reached by a fluke.

4

Most of us here have not yet reached the middle state — that condition where the heart cries day and night for the Lord. No, not yet. How to reach that state is the question. As I said, the first part of this devotional venture is formal; that is to say, we have to go through all kinds of formal practices. We do not even know whether the feelings that come into our heart are trustworthy or not. Don't bother about it. This is a stage in which there is a great deal of struggle, and in struggle, one isn't always able to measure what is right and what is wrong, which emotion is genuine and which is spurious. Just follow your own ideal, and gradually you will come out of this uncertain stage.

Some of the important elements in formal practice are worship of the Lord; keeping the company of devotees — if you can find devotees, and if they will allow you to keep their company; reading of the scriptures, of the lives of saints and sages; repeating the name of God; singing His glory; meditating upon Him; and serving the children of God. Now, these are essential elements. Don't think that you can just pick and choose there. You have to do *all* of them. According to your need and temperament you may do one more than the others, but all of them you will have to do. You cannot say, 'Oh, yes, I love God, but I hate people; I don't care for them.' Remember that classification I mentioned? Only the lowest kind of devotee would do that. But then you do not want to remain in the lowest grade always; so you will have to mend your ways. You will have to learn to like everybody and serve everybody. And then when you do all these things consistently day after day, gradually great love of God will come into your heart.

Lest some of you have this question in your mind, I shall mention that these devotional practices pre-suppose a pure, moral life. If you say that your mind is not completely free of immoral tendencies, of worldly tendencies, then I say, try to live your life in the best way you can; restrain yourself, live at least externally a pure life, and as you practise devotion you will find that worldly tendencies lose their vigour. Just as when you do not water or feed the roots of plants they are gradually starved, in the same way, when you have withdrawn your interest from worldly things and have directed it towards God, gradually worldly tendencies, being devoid of nourishment, die out. And just as when you light a lamp in a dark room darkness vanishes, in the same way when love of God grows even in a slight degree in your heart then all those worldly tendencies disappear. Just as darkness is the lack of light, so worldly tendencies, although they seem to be positive things, really speaking are negative; they're the lack of love for God, and so, as this love of God grows in our heart, to that extent they disappear. But first you should deliberately cultivate moral and unworldly tendencies, because otherwise you will not have even the beginning of love in your heart. You start this way, and very soon you find that by sheer practice of devotion you have become free of all worldliness; your mind has become purified and unified, and out of that will come a spontaneous longing for God.

GOD AND GOD-MEN IN VEDANTA

1

Vedanta of course believes in God, but the ideas of God that are taught in the Vedanta philosophy and religion are sometimes difficult to comprehend. For example, the idea that God is without any attributes, beyond mind, beyond even the grasp of reason and intelligence seems to many to indicate a sort of agnosticism, because if God is without attributes and if He cannot be reached by the human mind or comprehended by the human intellect, then how can anyone know whether or not He exists? He who is beyond the reach of mind and thought and intelligence is, in fact, as good as nonexistent. That is one of the things that puzzle many who want to study Vedanta.

But having proposed such a God, Vedanta then speaks of God *with* attributes, and, as such, it speaks of Him as being the creator and preserver and destroyer of the universe — which seems rather a contradiction of the first proposition. And, in fact, there Vedantists sometimes halt and say, 'Yes, God exists and is endowed with all kinds of benign qualities, but we are not quite sure that He is the creator of this universe or that He has anything to do with it.' For example, in the *Brahma Sūtras* there is a very well-known discussion of how there can be suffering and evil in God's creation. The conclusion given is that God cannot be held responsible for any evil in this universe, because to ascribe evil to God is to deny the very essence of divine nature. So then they have to explain how all this evil and trouble came to be.

Sometimes Vedanta philosophers go to the other extreme. They say that God is responsible for the evil as well as for the good in this universe. They sometimes go so far as to say that everything here is an expression of divinity; whether it seems to be living or nonliving, good or evil, pleasant or unpleasant — everything is an expression of God. To our common sense that seems to be an impossible proposition, and yet that is exactly what they maintain. Another somewhat puzzling idea is that while God is considered to be formless, Vedanta speaks of Him as having form; sometimes in the ancient books the forms of God are even described. How can it be that God, who is infinite and formless, as Vedanta more often says, is at the same time endowed with form?

These are of course great puzzles and have to be explained. And I should tell you here that all these divergent and apparently contradictory ideas of God, which were originally presented in the Vedanta texts, the Upanishads, were confusing even to the ancient students of this philosophy; in fact, we find that great efforts were made by our philosophers and sages to find a harmony among them. So it may be useful if I dwell briefly on the Vedantic ideas of God, and I shall do so later on. But in choosing my subject I had in mind a very particular topic — the relationship between God and God-men as it is explained by our philosophy.

Let me first of all define the term *God-man* as we understand it. You see, in the Hindu religious tradition we believe that many people have become saints, that is to say, actual knowers of God. We have also conceived the knowledge of God to be of different degrees and stages, so that if you have the insight to see into the mind of a spiritual man, you will at once know what degree or stage of spiritual growth he has attained. Some have truly seen God, and to see God is no easy thing. It is said that it takes many lifetimes, many incarnations as human beings, for the soul to reach a state where it craves for God essentially, and that state is only the precondition of spiritual experience. When a person feels within himself that he doesn't want anything of the outside world, when the greater part of his aspiration is directed towards God, when he is convinced in his heart of hearts that God is the essential truth, that He is the abode of all goodness, and that to find Him is to be fulfilled completely and everlastingly — when this condition is reached, one is able to travel towards God. And it is then, after having practised meditation and dwelt upon God with all one's heart and soul, that one comes so close to Him as to actually see Him. That is the first experience of God we have.

But you see, that is only the beginning, because the soul, not being satisfied with the first glimpse of God, travels further towards Him and becomes, you might say, unified with Him—not identified, but unified. The soul still feels itself as distinct from God but very close to Him; there is nothing now between itself and God. We believe that last of all comes complete absorption of the soul in God. In that absorption the soul is not lost but becomes completely identified with God; the divine consciousness becomes his own consciousness, and the two consciousnesses are not separate or even distinct. This is the way the soul travels towards God and has the highest vision of God.

It is maintained that when a person has only the first vision of God, he still retains his own individuality, in which there are likes and dislikes and limitations, but when such a person becomes more and more merged in God, then many of his human aspects drop off. A little remains of them, but they become so transformed that rarely can you call him an ordinary human being. You may call him a saint, if you use the word *saint* to imply that he or she has had the direct vision of God. We Hindus have many other words to designate such a person. For example, you are well acquainted with the term *mahātmā*, the term that was applied to Mahatma Gandhi. *Mahātmā*

means 'great soul' — that is to say, one who has
shed the limitations of an ordinary individual and
has become *maha*, 'great'. *Maha* indicates not only
greatness of quality but also greatness of dimension;
there is a largeness about such a person, and it is
that intangible largeness that is specifically indicated
by this word *maha*. It does not always mean 'noble
soul', as it is sometimes translated. It means 'great
soul', because that soul is great, literally great.

There is another term, however, which seems to
be more appropriate and is more commonly used. It
is *mahapuruṣa*. *Mahāpuruṣa* literally means 'great
man', but it conveys the sense that the person has
become infinite; having become related to this
infinite Being, God, he is no longer a small individual,
a small *puruṣa*. We apply this title to a person who,
we know, has become more or less united with God.
His very appearance indicates that there has taken
place within him a profound transformation. We
notice his ways: his needs, his appetites, his likes, his
ways of sleeping and eating — all these things have
changed, they no longer have any similarity to those
of an ordinary person.

We find, however, that amongst these *mahāpuruṣas*, these saints or great souls, there are some
who seem to enjoy a position that is given to them
not so much by men as by God. For instance, in the
Semitic tradition a prophet is not merely a saint; he
has a divine function to fulfil. He is, as it were, the
messenger of God to His children; he is inspired,

and he brings something from above for the good of the people amongst whom he is born. They have a spiritual authority, these prophets: people seem to take to them and to their teachings almost spontaneously; there is no coercion about it. In India, also, we have recognized amongst our saints and sages some who seem to have a special function.

Shankara, for example, was a great philosopher, probably the greatest born in India, and at the same time he was a very great saint; he was a unique combination of the highest spiritual experience and the highest philosophical genius. Yet he is looked upon not as an Incarnation, but as a saint with authority, one who was born for the good of mankind. He lived just thirty-two years, and then, his mission fulfilled, he passed on.

Ramanuja, who is not considered to equal Shankara in importance, fulfilled a similar function — that is, he is considered to be a man with spiritual authority. Greater saints may have been born in India, but they have not enjoyed the same authority as has Ramanuja. Unlike Shankara, he was a theist, that is to say, a devotee of God. Although Shankara was also a devotee of God, at the same time he was a monist, feeling that he himself and every other being was identical with God. Ramanuja, on the other hand, emphasized the soul's devotional relationship with God, and so he described God in one particular way. Later on, I shall have occasion to refer to his view.

Now, if you consider all the saints of this class, all the *mahāpuruṣas*, you find that some enjoy the *greatest* authority. Not only are they saints, not only are they men of God — they have also become God-men. And some God-men — for example, Sri Krishna or Buddha or Sri Ramakrishna — are so great that you find the so-called man aspect, human aspect, is almost gone: there remains in them God and nothing but God. Such God-men have been called Divine Incarnations.

Of course, as you can well understand, there has been a great deal of controversy amongst the Hindus about whether the idea of Divine Incarnation is legitimate or not. At the very outset, who are those who can call a God-man or a saint an Incarnation of God? If we call someone a Divine Incarnation, that might be awfully nice of us, indicating that we feel a great deal of devotion towards him, but that does not *prove* anything. After all, we are ignorant people. Once a disciple of Buddha began to praise him in his presence. He said, 'There has never been so glorious a person as you.' Well, Buddha, who never liked this kind of flattery, just said, 'I imagine you have known all the Buddhas at the present time?' 'No, sir.' 'Maybe you knew all the Buddhas of the past?' 'No.' 'Of the future?' 'No.' 'Then how can you say this?' Well, a similar question arises: How do you know that a saint, or a *mahāpuruṣa*, is an Incarnation of God? It's a very difficult question to answer, and I may frankly tell you that probably never will this question be answered to the satisfaction of all or of even a large number of people. It will always remain problematical.

2

There are, however, certain specialities ascribed to a Divine Incarnation (of course, whether a given saint has these specialities, it would be very difficult to prove or disprove). One special mark is that he has no ordinary history of previous lives. Whereas it is assumed that an ordinary soul has gone through many births and has suffered from many kinds of disabilities in the course of its spiritual evolution, the Divine Incarnation has a divine history; he may say, 'Yes, I was incarnated as Christ in such and such a time; now I am incarnated as this.' That is to say, his history is always the history of a Divine Incarnation and never the history of an ignorant man.

Another speciality maintained of Divine Incarnations is that while we find that they have struggled to attain to God and may approach God or talk about Him as if they were ordinary devotees seeking His mercy — crying for Him, feeling their separation from Him — all those things are only playacting on their part; actually speaking, they are always conscious that they are God Himself.

Further, it is thought that from their very birth Divine Incarnations are aware that they are born for a certain purpose. For instance, it is said of Buddha that as soon as he was born he at once recognized that his mother would not live long enough to hear the message of enlightenment that he had come to give to mankind; so then and there he preached to her the Dharma, the Law. Now, you might say that's a legend. Well, it may be a legend, but at least it indicates the underlying idea of a Divine Incarnation as maintained by the faithful. It indicates that even as a newborn baby, the Divine Incarnation knows he is God, and baby or no baby, he behaves like the omniscient and omnipotent Person that God is considered to be. Of Sri Krishna, also, we find a similar story. When he was born in a prison cell he at once became luminous and began to give teachings to his parents. You know the story of how Krishna's uncle had been told that one of the children of his own sister would kill him; so immediately after his sister's marriage he put both her and her husband in prison. As children were born to them, he took infant after infant and killed it. Now, when the Lord Himself was born, the parents felt immeasurably attracted to Him. Wherever there is anything of God we feel attracted; that's the idea. So the parents felt a particularly great attraction for this child and were very much frightened that he, too, would be killed; therefore he assumed his divine form to reassure them. We find these stories again and again in connection with those who have been looked upon as Incarnations of God.

There is another special mark: when Divine

204 MEDITATION, ECSTASY, AND ILLUMINATION

Incarnations begin to function they are capable of granting anything they want; there is no limit to it. One thing specifically they grant to men is forgiveness of sin. In the Jewish tradition forgiveness was a special function of God, and so the Jews — at least those who considered Christ to be only a man and not the promised Messiah — were scandalized when they heard that he would forgive the sins of others. In India we seldom use the word sin; more often we say that a Divine Incarnation can break the bonds of *karma*. He can say to someone, 'All right, your *karmas* are broken now; you have become free.'

We all know how difficult it is to change ourselves. We find old forms of thought coming back to us; we think we have gotten rid of them, but they have a mysterious way of reasserting themselves from time to time, and all our years of struggle seem to have meant nothing. There is a persistence about these habits of thought. But when a Divine Incarnation says, 'All right, all this is gone' — it's gone. It's such an extraordinary thing! Sometimes, just by a word, a touch, or a glance they can reveal before you, then and there, the vision of God — a thing for which people ordinarily struggle life after life. It is as though a far-off uncle, long forgotten, suddenly appears on the scene, maybe from Australia. He is full of money, and he leaves a tremendous fund for his nephews and nieces, and thenceforth they are rich. God brings that tremendous fund of spiritual blessings and redemptive power to the human level. This, in fact, is the whole idea behind the Divine Incarnation.

Such powers are not possessed by prophets. Prophets have a great influence on people; they can so strongly impress many minds with certain thoughts that they create a following, and thereby a sect is formed. Even after a prophet has gone, a group of people follow his ways of thinking through centuries. But you know, to follow ways of thinking is one thing and to enjoy the fruits of such thinking is quite another. The world is full of sects and creeds, and each goes its own way. But do you mean to say that all their followers derive benefit from them? Many people want to come closer to God, but by following these sects how many are able to actually feel His proximity? Prophets may institute new modes of worship, new modes of thinking; they may give commandments and say, 'You should not do this, you should do this', but that peculiar power which for centuries and centuries inspires people to practise these teachings so wholeheartedly that their efforts become immediately effective, bringing about changes in their lives, that power belongs to the Divine Incarnation; it is not given to the prophets. In short, Divine Incarnations alone have the tremendous power of redemption. You are absolutely right in thinking, if you are a Christian, that Christ was the Redeemer. This is what is meant by 'Redeemer': he who can break away the opposing forces and bring out the graces of the soul — that is, he who grants salvation. Christ did that.

Further we find that a Divine Incarnation, before he passes on, leaves that special power with those of his apostles or disciples who are fitted for it, and they in turn give some of their power to *their* disciples. It is found that this redeeming power works for generations with astonishing effectiveness. But we maintain — this is the tradition in India — that even the power of a Divine Incarnation has an end. Generally the belief is that under normal conditions it goes on working with very tangible effectiveness for, say, five centuries, and we have noticed, in India at least, that for five centuries it *does* go on, then comes a decline, and then appears another Incarnation of God. By now, we almost expect it to happen like that. But you see, about God you cannot say anything; there is no compulsion about Him that He has to appear every five hundred years.

Anyhow, the power does decline, and one reason is that there are no longer proper channels for it. After several generations, the disciples become impure, they become worldly minded; that single-minded devotion to God falls away. Just as a stream of clear water flows freely through new pipes for several years and then dwindles because the pipes have become clogged or have rusted and sprung leaks, in the same way the dispensation of a Divine Incarnation comes to an end because the generations of disciples that follow him become rusted; they are no longer pure and clear channels. It is no use having just a mechanical belief: the Redeemer came, and whether his followers are saints or scoundrels, it doesn't matter, they become equally good channels of the divine power. If God really is so indiscriminate about moral and spiritual virtues, then why, when He became incarnated as, say, Christ, did He teach moral virtues? Why did He teach purity? Why did He teach spiritual virtues? Why did He say that if you want God, you must give up everything, you must love Him with your whole mind, whole heart, and whole soul? Such teachings mean that you cannot live in proximity to God, you cannot feel His nearness, unless you become the right instrument. In India that is what we believe, and therefore we do not care a fig for those who say they are in direct line of discipleship of a Divine Incarnation unless they themselves are fit.

Now, there is another speciality about Divine Incarnations. It is found that they actually fulfil the need of their times. That is an astonishing thing about them. What a people have knowingly or unknowingly been seeking as the fulfilment of an ideal becomes realized in the Divine Incarnation. And then, if a people think about him and contemplate the teachings he gave, they come closer and closer to the realization of that ideal. A prophet or a saint is not so comprehensive; he doesn't represent the total ideal for which a certain age is struggling. These, then, are several special things about Divine Incarnations.

We find that Christian ideas on this subject are almost parallel to the ideas that we have been entertaining in India. As you know, only these two religions — Christianity and Hinduism — believe in the Incarnation of God, and we find that the underlying idea in both religions is that, although God is everywhere, men because of their human nature, in which there is a great deal of limitation and impurity, are not able to apprehend Him. Man's mind is so intractable that it is very difficult — I should say almost impossible — for him to change his mind or his nature by his own effort. What is the answer to it? As we look at human history, we always find two forces working: just as evil flourishes here, good also flourishes; just as there are some minds that go downhill, there are other minds continually climbing upwards. That's the glory of human nature — on the whole it never admits defeat. We always find men and women who represent in their lives those ideals after which we aspire, and such men and women become a source of great encouragement to us. In the case of a Divine Incarnation, of course, the ideal becomes a million times more magnified and real. There God Himself is visible; therefore it is said that the purpose of a Divine Incarnation is to make the invisible God visible, the hidden God present before us. It is as though God in His infinite mercy had come to our normal mind to be known and perceived by it. Psychologically speaking, a normal mind cannot perceive God; it is too limited and crude. And yet God comes closer to this normal mind, so that without much effort on its part it is able to feel His presence. You see, that is one of the reasons God becomes incarnated. And that is a very extraordinary thing.

Let me repeat myself: One way we can know God is through bringing about a profound change in our mind through meditation and other spiritual practices so that we become ready to perceive Him, but that is a very difficult task; so God comes to our own level. He rises, as it were, from some profound depths of reality and comes up to the surface where we dwell; He makes Himself known to us and felt by us. We cannot resist Him any more. We feel His peace, we feel His joy, we feel His great love. He becomes like a man amongst us. He showers His blessings upon us. He shows that He doesn't take any offence at anything, He forgets all our faults, all the wrong things we have done; He ignores them. He just says, 'Go and sin no more' — finished! With a gracious smile He breaks the bondages of our soul and grants us freedom. And we find, also, that in our distress and difficulties He comes and grants us security, rescues us from difficulty. All these things He does, and it becomes real to us that He is indeed the one who loves us most. If a person were to come to you and say, 'Don't worry; in life or in death, in safety or in danger I shall forever abide by you' — if someone says that and proves it from time to time, wouldn't you think the greatest thing had happened to you and wouldn't your whole heart go to such a person? You could never forget him. You see, a Divine Incarnation does that; he comes and he gives all these assurances to us. A prophet or a saint may give you advice, he may help you by watching over you, and so on, but he can't say, 'All right, I shall take all your difficulties away this moment; don't worry.' He just doesn't have the authority to say that. But a Divine Incarnation can say all those things. That is one difference.

The *basic* differences between a Divine Incarnation and a prophet or saint, however, are those which I mentioned first: Divine Incarnations do not have an ordinary history; they have always been Incarnations of God, they always remember themselves to be God; they always know that they have come to this world with a mission. And from time to time they manifest their divine nature in power as well as in compassion and love and wisdom. These are the basic demarcations.

3

Now, when you ask a Vedantist, 'What is your idea about these people? Do you recognize these special qualities and powers?' some will say, 'Of course!' Earlier I mentioned Ramanuja. His interpretation of Vedanta, for example, is called qualified monistic Vedanta. It is not pure monism; it is qualified, modified. He always maintained that there is a distinction, I might almost say a difference, between the individual soul and the universal soul, God. He said that even in the ultimate state, even when the individual soul has realized itself in its true nature and is not suffering from ignorance or bondage — even then it will find itself to be distinct from God. Whereas God is infinite and eternal, is endowed with an infinite number of benign qualities, and never undergoes any kind of change in the sense of losing or forgetting His divine nature, the individual soul undergoes changes in the sense of contraction and expansion — Ramanuja uses these two words. He says when the soul suffers from ignorance and impurity it contracts; and when a person has undertaken certain spiritual practices and thereby has filled himself with love and devotion, he becomes free from impurity and ignorance and his soul expands. But even that expansion is limited compared with God. That is Ramanuja's idea; so according to him, Divine Incarnations of course have special qualities and powers; the question of whether or not there is a difference between them and prophets or saints simply does not arise.

The question does arise, however, amongst the followers of monistic Vedanta who admit no distinction or difference between the individual soul and God. They argue in this way: 'You are making too much of the difference between, say, a prophet on one side and a Divine Incarnation on the other. You start with an idea of human nature which may not be altogether true: you think human nature is limited. Is that a right assumption?' Some Vedantists will ask that. As you know, one of the great teachings of the Vedanta philosophy, particularly of its monistic school, is that man is not really man, he is the infinite, eternal Divinity; that is his true nature. Because we have forgotten our true nature, we appear to be endowed with a body and a mind and to be limited by them — not only limited by them, we think we *are* the body and the mind — at least the mind. But suppose you think 'I am not this body, I am not this mind' and thereby take away whatever limitations the body and mind are imposing upon you, and suppose that in the same way you take from God His creativity and all other attributes, then you and God become one; you will not be able to distinguish one from the other in the slightest. As Shankara said, if you take the kingdom from a king and the shield from a soldier, how will you distinguish one from the other? It is only when, in your present conception, you think of God as endowed with creative powers and with this and that, and when you think of yourself as limited and suffering from such limitations, that you are the common soldier and He is the king.

Now, you might object, 'That is just a trick of thought. Say you are able to divest yourself of body and mind, but let us see how you divest God of His creative power! What can you do to God? He may say, "I won't allow you to take My creative power from Me." Then how will you become one with Him?' Of course, there are answers to these questions, but I won't go into them here. Suffice it to say that there are many instances in which God has been realized

as the Absolute, the indescribable, where there is no
question of creation and therefore no question of any
kind of power. When there is no other reality, or
individuals to dominate, to create or destroy, to be
kind or cruel to — when none of those things are there,
then none of these powers are there — all gone; that is
the Absolute Divinity. You who do not want to be
always looking at this universe, always aware of it,
and therefore pestered by it — you have the power of
transcending it; you reach a point where the whole
universe of phenomena has been left behind, and
there you meet God. God also has no universe to
rule at that time, and you feel absolutely identified
with Him. There is nothing to distinguish you from
God or God from you. This fact has been so well
recognized that even in the most ancient times in
India, when this philosophy began to take shape
and form, the general view was: *brahma veda
brahmaiva bhavati*[1] — 'He who knows Brahman
becomes Brahman.' They just said it point-blank. You
see, in that state, the distinctions between saints,
prophets, and Incarnations are all wiped away. The
question is, have you known God enough? That's the
point. And if you say, 'Yes, I know Him enough; I
have come so close to Him, I have become one with
Him; I am not merely united with Him, I have
become identified with Him; there is nothing to
distinguish me from Him, not even a thin line

---

[1] *Muṇḍaka Upaniṣad,* 3. 2. 9.

separates me from Him' — if you have realized that, then you can't be called either a saint or a prophet or an Incarnation. According to these thinkers there is no distinction there at all.

To that, the answer given by those monists who believe in Divine Incarnations is, 'Oh, all right, if you are talking about that state where all become one, we shall say that there is no question of Divine Incarnation or of anything else. But what about the relative plane? Suppose some who have realized their identity with God come down to this phenomenal universe — are there not differences amongst them? Do not some have a more impressive nature? Are not some more able to help others, some who feel the sufferings and the needs of people more keenly and respond more effectively than others? Some do indeed serve the purpose of an age more than the others. These are facts and therefore you have to admit them. Otherwise, you thinkers would not be thinking rightly. And if you recognize these differences, would you not, then, use different terms in relation to different kinds of saints and sages, calling some Divine Incarnations?'

Well, of course, the opponents might. But they would say, 'What difference does it make? On the phenomenal level differences are always there. That is what creation is; everybody is different from everybody else, and if you make much of these differences of power you are not propounding a new principle, you are only affirming, in regard to saints, the same principle of differences and distinctions, which seems to be the very basis of creation. What new thing are you saying?' But, you see, the point is that some saints do make a *basic* distinction. If you ask them, 'What was your past birth?' they would not say, 'In my past lives I struggled, and this time I have become perfect.' They never say that. They will probably say, 'Previously I was born as such and such a Divine Incarnation.' Or they will say, 'I didn't have any past history.' That is where the real fight comes in.

As I have told you, we find that in ancient times a sage would realize his complete identity with God. Now, sometimes someone among such sages would say, 'I am the Lord of the universe; it is through my power that everybody functions as he does. The gods have been created through my power', or sometimes, 'I have become the sun and the moon'. They would say that kind of thing. And of course those are tremendous statements. You may think they were indulging in imagination, as poets do — getting into a sort of frenzy and saying things that should not be taken literally but should just be enjoyed. But our philosophers have not held that view; they have taken these claims to be literally true. And you must remember here that when people progress in spiritual life, some *do* come to this kind of experience. They call it the experience of the *Bhuman*, the experience of the Vast One. They realize themselves as this Infinite One. Now, would you not call such people

Divine Incarnations? That's the point. Strangely enough, however, such people were not called Divine Incarnations in those early days. It was only later that that idea took shape in India.

When we think of the history of the doctrine of Divine Incarnation, we find that while the philosophy of monistic Vedanta, of the identity of the soul with Brahman, was developing, not merely through speculation — I should say least of all through speculation — but through contemplation and direct experience, the idea of Divine Incarnation was also developing. It must have taken at least two to three thousand years to formulate monistic ideas in India. You see, without any help, without any precedents, those ancient sages had to grope their way into a truth about which they had never even heard anything. Somebody had to be the first to find it, and that kind of finding takes a long, long time. Well, while this was going on, several parallel developments were also taking place. One was of the Bhagavata religion — the worship of the *Bhagavān*. The *Bhagavān* is one who is endowed with all kinds of glories; He is not only the Creator, Preserver, and Destroyer, He is also the beloved Lord of the heart, the Compassionate One. He is the Lord who is worshipped today by the devotees of many different religions — Christianity, for example. One of the ideas embodied in this Bhagavata religion was the idea of the Divine Incarnation. We do not know when that idea first originated; it was there in India at an early time, although it did not take prominent form until much later. Let me here refer to a book which is considered to be one of the most authoritative scriptures of this school — the *Bhagavad-Gītā*, which was written long before the Christian era. There we find that the doctrine of Divine Incarnation has taken very clear form and is well enunciated. Sri Krishna, who gives this teaching, is himself the *Bhagavān*; he is the Lord, the Glorious One, and he is also considered to be the Incarnation of the Lord.

Now, monistic Vedantists, as you know, are very accommodating: they do not want to deny any fact or truth; they make room for it in their scheme of things; therefore, the idea of Divine incarnation gradually became a part of Vedanta philosophy. In fact, although the *Bhagavad-Gītā* is a scripture of the Bhāgavata school, it has also been considered one of the authoritative texts of Vedanta. And in the *Gītā*, as I have just told you, the doctrine of Divine Incarnation is clearly enunciated; so that doctrine became acceptable to Vedanta.

4

One could say that in regard to the doctrine of Divine Incarnation two schools of monistic Vedanta developed. As I have pointed out, the followers of one school say that every soul is destined to realize its identity with Brahman one day and that the idea of an ultimate distinction between the soul and God, such as is maintained by most religious people, is false; don't even consider it. They say, suppose you realize your identity with God, truly realize your identity with God, and then come down to a relative level and find the old limitations coming back to you in greater or lesser degree — resist those limitations! Affirm your true divine, infinite nature even on the relative plane, and go on affirming it. Let us see what expansion takes place within you! There is a view that if such a person practises that way, then, although he lives on the relative plane, a profound change takes place in him; he is no longer just a man. He does not say, 'Well, of course, as long as I live on the relative plane I have my limitations, apparent limitations, but when I go into deep meditation I become God-like.' No. They say that if he continually affirms his identity with Brahman, gradually his nature expands and there comes an infinitude in him. And such a person, even living on the relative plane, may manifest divine nature from time to time. That is the attitude of a follower of the uncompromising school of monistic Vedanta.

Others say, 'Well, that's fine if he does it, but generally speaking, he doesn't do it, and therefore we recognize this distinction: a Divine Incarnation is someone apart; let us accept it as a practical fact. We worship him, we love him, and we are benefited by him, because he has overflowing power for our own good. For our own benefit he comes amongst us. Why should we struggle against that fact?'

The followers of the first school do not recognize Divine Incarnation in the accepted sense; they just say, 'Yes, you become one with God, and when you become one with God you *are* one with God; no doubt can be raised.' And if you point out that on the relative plane there are distinctions and differences amongst those who have already realized that identity, they say yes, on the relative plane there are these differences, but they need not be accepted as permanent. If, for instance, you find that someone is manifesting more divinity than you are, then go on breaking all your limitations; you will also manifest more divinity if you like.

I myself have witnessed the truth of this. I had the good fortune of living with many knowers of God. I and others knew them through the years, and one of the most beautiful things we noticed was that although they were knowers of God even in their youth, as time went on there came a sort of expansion of their being. In several cases the expansion was so great that almost within one year their personality seemed to have totally changed; they manifested qualities much greater than those who had earlier been considered greater than they. Tremendous expansion took place. Tremendous! Now, how do you account for that? The only way you can account for it is by admitting that if your mind dwells in that higher plane, the divine plane, and you resist the limitations contrary to divine nature, then even though you may live on the relative plane, gradually you will find that a more expansive nature, which is essentially divine, begins to assert itself. Powers come, ability comes; if such a person says something it will be fulfilled. So, you see, some Vedantists say, 'How can you distinguish such people from a Divine Incarnation? They *are* Incarnations.'

Swami Vivekananda once enunciated a principle by which you can distinguish Divine Incarnations from other saints and sages. He said that they are characterized by tremendous compassion, and he designated as Incarnations of God some saints who had never before been looked upon as such and spoke of one or two who *have* been looked upon as Divine Incarnations as just saints or prophets or scholars.[2] Now, of course, the majority won't agree with that assessment of his, but when a Swami Vivekananda makes a statement in connection with such subjects, his words have to be accepted for at least serious consideration. Anyhow, his criterion was compassion. The heart of a person becomes so large, he feels so at one with all, that you cannot distinguish him from an Incarnation. Even if originally you didn't think him to be an Incarnation, he has now become like one, and when he is *like*, then he *is*. You cannot stick to 'like' for long, you see. You begin to ask, 'Why do I call him *like* ? The right substance is there: real compassion, endless compassion, is there; so why should I say it is *like*

---

2. *The Complete Works of Swami Vivekananda*, 6:393-94 (9th edition).

universal compassion? It is the same universal compassion that is ascribed to a Divine Incarnation.'

But as I said, Vedantists don't want to deny any fact or truth. So if you aren't an extreme monist, that is to say, if you aren't absorbed in contemplation of the attributeless Brahman — Brahman beyond anything that is relative — then you will find that the idea of Divine Incarnation as someone apart has a great deal of practical justification; you can easily accept it. From a theoretical standpoint, also, there is no difficulty about the concept of Divine Incarnation, if you think, as do all Vedantists of whatever school, that there is an *Īśvara* or God, a Lord of this universe.

This brings me to the various and contradictory ideas of God in Vedanta that I mentioned at the outset. You see, our philosophers have reconciled them by recognizing that they represent different experiences of God in different stages of spiritual awareness. They are all true. To put it briefly: if you are approaching God from a lower state, your first knowledge of Him is not intimate. Just as on first acquaintance with a great man we do not know much about his inner life, so our first knowledge of God — not theoretical knowledge, but knowledge through direct perception — is not complete. But when you come closer to God and know Him more intimately, then you find He is a little different than you had thought Him to be. And I may say here that the last or highest knowledge that you have of God is as the Lord of Love. All creation can be left behind. You just feel that He is the beloved Lord of your heart and you are His loving devotee, that only the two of you have remained. That is *Īśvara*. In a lower vision you find that He is the Creator; He is the Maintainer; He is also the Lord of compassion; He is seated in the heart of our hearts as our Inner Regulator—the Soul of our soul. He regulates our destiny, He grants salvation, He also regulates the moral law in the universe. As a matter of fact, at every stage the whole universe—whether it is the material world, the living world, the moral world, or the spiritual world—is governed by God, by His will. You have all these visions of God, and *Īśvara* is the highest, or as monists would say, *Īśvara* is the highest view of God short of identity with the Absolute.

So when Vedantists think of God as *Īśvara* they see nothing contradictory in the idea of Divine Incarnation. He who is the Lord of Love, He who is our Father and Mother and Friend and Lord and Beloved, why should He not come amongst us as our very own, live amongst us and call us His children or His friends, teach us, and make us taste His affection and His love? What is there wrong in it? Rather, if you think as Vedantists think, you should say that this whole universe is a self-expression of the Lord through His joy. In one of the discourses of the Upanishads it is said that it is from joy that the universe came into being. *Ānandāddhyeva khalvimāni bhūtāni jāyante ...* [3] — 'Verily, from joy all beings

---

[3.] *Taittirīya Upaniṣad,* 3. 6. 1.

have come into existence; by joy, having come into existence, they are maintained; and into joy they dissolve.' So if this universe is a self-expansion of the Lord in joy, why should we wonder that on this very earth, which is also part of that self-manifestation, He might not sometimes appear as a man amongst men and look at us and say, 'Hello!'? I think that is to be expected.

There is a beautiful picture of Christ in which he is shown knocking at a door. If you can think of the Son of God knocking at your door, why can you not think of God Himself doing that? If the Son of God can do it, God also can do it. He comes sometimes and makes us feel that we are still His children; we can look to Him, and whatever we ask of Him He will grant us. Sri Ramakrishna continually taught this, 'Don't forget that you are Her children'—just as Christ often spoke of God as Father, Sri Ramakrishna spoke of God as Mother. He said, 'Remember, we are Her own children, not stepchildren and not adopted children. She has actually given birth to us, and therefore, just as children have a claim on the mother, why don't you claim your birthright from the Divine Mother? You are Her children—claim it!' Well, if we are not one of those who feel that they are not body and mind but pure, flaming Spirit and who become one with this blazing fire which is called Brahman without attributes—if we are not one of those, then why should we not expect God to come amongst us, respond to us, and allow us to approach Him through our human nature? Such Vedantists say, 'It's quite all right if He comes; the more the merrier.'

After all, everyone is an Incarnation of God; that is to say, Brahman has taken a body. Even the extreme Vedantists will say, *jīva brahmaiva nāparaḥ*[4] – 'The individual is nothing else but Brahman.' And if this extreme Vedantist is true to his own philosophy, he will look upon every face and say, 'This is the face of Brahman.' He may not say 'Beloved Lord', he may not use those melting terms, but he still will say, 'Everyone is really Brahman – *Saccidānanda*, Being-Consciousness-Bliss Absolute – appearing in these forms.' And if someone can reply, 'Yes, I am That; you too. Come, let us play. You are Brahman, I am also Brahman', that would be better still, wouldn't it?

Once Sri Ramakrishna said of an experience of his that suddenly a boy came out of his body, a sixteen-year-old boy with a shining form; he also became a sixteen-year-old boy, and the two began to run and play for a long time. He said there came a mist of joy; the whole world vanished away, and they played like this. You might think that was some kind of fantasy. Nothing of the kind. Divine nature has a tendency to see Itself magnified in infinite forms. That is what creation is. He is the One, He sees Himself reflected in an infinite number of forms; that is His joy. Just as a vain person will surround

---

4. Shankara, *Brahmajñānavalīmālā*, 21.

himself with mirrors, look at his reflections all around him, and admire his eyebrows or lips or eyes and curl his hair like this or like that — that is what the Lord is doing. That's the great fun.

You think that only the foolish enjoy such fun? Everybody is doing it; you understand another person to the extent that you see yourself reflected there. Do you see anything more than your own reflection in another person? You don't. That is why Christ said, 'Judge not that ye be not judged.' When you say, 'There is a bad man', you are saying, 'The badness of my mind is comprehending the badness there', and thereby you are being judged. You are not judging the other person, you are judging as much of yourself as you can catch in the other form. *Everything* is one's own reflection, a judgement of oneself. Can you deny this? If you think deeply, you *cannot* deny it.

That is the mystery of the whole creation: we are the One. We are seeing the dead part of our being as matter, dead matter. The ferocious part we are seeing as tigers and lions and so on. There is a good part also; we are seeing it as saints. That is what is happening. If you go deep, deep down and investigate all the layers of your mind and see how consciousness functions in each of these levels, you will be astonished. Some part of this mind is creating this vast universe; another part is creating the gods. We are all seeing ourselves in so-called others. There are no others, there are just infinite

226 MEDITATION, ECSTASY, AND ILLUMINATION

forms projected, in which we have reflected ourselves; that is all we are doing. This is the idea.

So Vedantists say since everything is really an
incarnation of divinity, if some incarnation smiles
back at us and says, 'Yes, here I am; what do you
want? Come on!' then he becomes the Divine
Incarnation. And why not? Why not? All the talk
about prophets who laid down the law, all the
struggles, and all the conceptions that we are steeped
in ignorance — all these ideas belong to a lower vision
of ourselves — a lower vision which we can at this
moment discard, because everyone is capable of a
higher vision — *now*. Even the greatest sinner can say,
'Lord, I am a miserable sinner; I know You are my
only hope.' In that very statement the miserable sinner
has access to the higher vision. He may not use this
grand language, 'I am God', but when he says, 'You
are the only one I have', he is making the same
statement. So you see, anyone is capable of having a
higher vision, only he may use different language.
The moment he has that vision, the whole world
changes for him.

Why should we not have that vision? All this
talk about who created the world, who destroys
it — this is the talk of those who do not want higher
truths. But when they want divine truth they say, 'I
don't care whether You create or destroy or don't
create or destroy. I want *You*. Let us go and talk.
Come on! No creation this time!' That's the language
of the devotee's heart to God; and it is said that in

the Divine Incarnation that longing is fulfilled. There is a very beautiful conceit in this connection in Indian thought. It is said that God becomes incarnated not for sinners, but for already illumined souls. You see, when God takes human form, there is an intimacy in which the soul enjoys Him much more than in flights of ecstasy. And it is for these souls that God becomes incarnated. It is said that that is the most intimate purpose of a Divine Incarnation.

Well, Vedantists find that these ideas do not conflict with their philosophy unless they live where there is no form, no condition, no attributes — and there are some who are so immersed in contemplation of the Absolute that such things as Incarnations and communion and intimacy with God mean nothing to them. If you talk of Incarnation, they don't seem to ignite to that idea. But the rest of the Vedantists believe in Divine Incarnations and feel that these God-men are indispensable for most of us. It is all very well to talk about union with Brahman and identity with Him or about meditation and contemplation and concentration, but we who have not reached those states yet can see them only in a person who represents them in his own life. We can read descriptions in the books, but unless we see those things in concrete form, even such descriptions may be misleading.

I can say that that has been true in my case. I remember when as a boy I became interested in spiritual life many spiritual ideas and truths had one meaning for me, but when I came in contact with great saints I began to see different meanings. Concrete, living demonstrations of subtle truths and realities are given by these God-men, and therefore they are indispensable for the practical pursuit of Vedanta and, for that matter, of any religion. Vedantists therefore take to this idea, and they wish there were many more Incarnations, because then we would have many more impressive demonstrations.

So then, as I have said, Divine Incarnations have become an almost essential part of the Vedanta philosophy. But if you remember the exception that I have mentioned, you would not become fanatical about it. You would not say that without an Incarnation you can never have salvation. We never say that; it would be a libel against the greatness of human nature. Man has within himself the power to transcend all his weaknesses, and, given time, to become perfect, because that is his true nature. Truly speaking, whichever way you look at it, he is divine, fully and completely.

MEDITATION, ECSTASY, AND ILLUMINATION

1

I am sure you recognize that the three words of my title — meditation, ecstasy, and illumination — mark the different stages of spiritual attainment. Illumination has also been spoken of as enlightenment. Buddha, for instance, attained to illumination or enlightenment; that is how he became the Buddha, the Enlightened One. I think the significance of this word is that the supreme Truth or supreme Reality exists, but because of a certain darkness in our vision — that is to say, because of ignorance — we are not able to perceive this most wonderful thing. Through regulated spiritual effort, this darkness is removed from our consciousness or perception, and as it disappears, we become aware of the supreme Reality. When all darkness has been removed, when there is only light — that is called illumination. The word *illumination* indicates a subjective transformation, but it is also a statement of things as they are; it points to something that is always here, that is eternal, all-satisfying — something which is to be perceived and without perceiving which, we remain immersed in the darkness of ignorance. Illumination is the highest state, but before we reach it we pass through many other states which are all very exalted.

Ecstasy is one of those advanced spiritual states. Outwardly, this condition is marked by the stopping of the function of the senses. The person cannot speak; there seems to be a tremendous emotion surging within him which prevents him from speaking; he cannot hear, he cannot see anything, or if he hears and sees, it is only very vaguely. Inwardly, that is to say subjectively, ecstasy is a state of very great joy and also of love. If a person is a follower of the path of devotion, or *bhakti yoga*, then he will feel an upsurge of love for God. If he is following some other path, say *jñāna yoga*, the path of reason, this love may not surge within him, but he will feel a tremendous joy, a joy that sometimes becomes so intense that it is difficult for the body to contain it. If a person enters into that state in our presence, we cannot but be impressed by the wonderfulness of it. The person seems to be completely transformed: his whole body shines with an unearthly light; his face clearly indicates that there is going on within him, something not of this earth, something that every one of us would like to possess even to a slight degree.

Well, of course, you cannot reach this state, or similar states, unless there has taken place a profound transformation in your own being, and that is where meditation comes in. I think it would be well to speak here of meditation when it has been well developed within us, that is to say, in a quite pronounced form. Meditation has been described in various ways in our books, and since hundreds and thousands of people in every country have practised meditation, these descriptions are confirmed by their experiences. For example, in the *Gītā* there is the phrase *yathā dīpo nivātastho* [1] – 'a flame in a place where there is not the slightest movement of air and which therefore does not flicker'. You must have sometimes noticed a candle flame just standing still. It is inspiring indeed. As a matter of fact, anything that stands still, that doesn't have any movement, seems inspiring to a spiritual person; it will give him memories of spiritual experience, of a deep state of meditation. Again, speaking of this high state of meditation, there is a passage in one of the Upanishads: *vṛkṣa iva stabdho divi tiṣṭhatyekaḥ tenedam pūrṇam puruṣeṇa sarvam* [2] – 'This One is existent, changeless in the whole universe, like a tree completely still against the sky'. There are other illustrations – *tailadhārāvat anavicchinnaḥ*, 'like the flow of oil without any interruption'. When oil flows from one vessel to another continuously, it will give you the impression that there is no movement at all.

---

[1]. *Bhagavad-Gītā*, 6. 19.

[2]. *Śvetāśvatara Upaniṣad*, 3. 9.

Oil is heavy; therefore air cannot enter into it, so if you do not look at the vessels and look at only the column of oil, it will appear to be standing still.

The idea behind these illustrations is that ordinarily the mind is continually moving. Every moment there is a change in the mind, however slight it might be, and that movement is called a *vṛtti*. *Vṛtti* means 'becoming' or 'mood' or 'mode'. Now, the mind of a person who is not accustomed to meditation and who has not become very calm continually moves from one mode to another. It may be that the modes are only slightly different, but often you will notice that your mind jumps from one thing to a completely different thing. Through the practice of meditation or other efforts at quieting the mind, you find you can make the mind have the same kind of *vṛtti* from moment to moment; it does not change. When you have achieved that state, you have become well established in meditation.

Now, when meditation has progressed, you find that you have become somewhat separated from the body. At that time you will recognize that you used to feel as if you were in a room the walls of which were pressing in upon you. Just imagine what a horror it would be if you were living in a room and found the four walls coming towards you and ultimately pressing against you from all sides! Even the thought is frightening, and the experience certainly would be terrible. But that is exactly our present condition. This body is a room in which we are living.

I say 'we'. Who are we? We are the Self. Here I should remind you of one of the important teachings of our philosophy. We are, as it were, made up of three different entities: the physical body, then the mind — of course, truly speaking, we are not made up of the body or the mind, but in our ignorance we think so — and the third entity is our real Self. In Sanskrit we use the word *Atman*, which can be translated as 'the Self' or 'the Spirit'. The Spirit is different from the mind even at the mind's best, and of course it is different from the body. The Spirit is self-sustained, independent. It does not depend upon the mind or upon the body, and if you ask what its characteristics are — it is all-consciousness. If you think that without the cooperation of the mind there cannot be any consciousness within you — no! Rather, when your mind is sometimes conscious, that is because the light of the Self, which is all-consciousness, is reflecting itself there.

There can be no comparison between this all-conscious entity, the Spirit, and anything else. Mind is unconscious, body is unconscious. That the body is unconscious is proved by the fact that when it dies, immediately consciousness goes; you cannot say the body in itself has consciousness. And if you say the mind has consciousness, then how is it that you speak of the unconscious? Is it not a fact that part of the mind is really unconscious? If something is partly conscious and partly unconscious, then consciousness does not belong to it, it is not essential to its nature.

Consciousness is not essential to the mind: it comes and it goes; therefore, mind in itself is not conscious. That is the Vedantic view.

The Spirit is all-consciousness; It is the very essence of all perfection. Only the body and the mind represent the principles of limitation, and if Spirit is beyond this body and mind, It is unlimited. It is the infinite One. It is not made up of anything; therefore it cannot die or undergo any change. Only things having parts can die and undergo change. If it is just one thing, homogeneous Spirit, then of course It is imperishable; It is eternal, immortal. And in It are all kinds of perfections: infinite joy, infinite peace, infinite love — all are in the Spirit, and that most wonderful Spirit is our own true being. Everyone can say and should say, 'That is my nature. I am the perfect Being.'

If you ask, 'How can I say that? I don't feel it', well, you say many things you don't feel. Just analyse the words you use in the course of a day; most of them don't mean anything to you in your experience; yet you are continually using these words. Why not say, 'I am the Spirit, this perfect Spirit'? We are so conscientious when it comes to spiritual things! The very soul of honesty and truth! In everyday life we cheat others and cheat ourselves all the time — not deliberately, but we use wrong words, think wrong thoughts; the whole thing is a mess! About that we do not bat an eye, but when it comes to spiritual matters, oh, we have to be very cautious! That is called confusion. What we should say, we don't say, and what we shouldn't say, that is what we say. That is one of the signs of ignorance.

In our present stage the body and the mind have impinged themselves so hard upon our Spirit that they seem to have squeezed it out of existence. So if you are asked, 'Don't you think you are the immortal Spirit?' you become very thoughtful — at least you try to *look* thoughtful, to *become* thoughtful is a big job — and you say, 'I don't feel any kind of Spirit. Body I can feel and also a little of the mind. Spirit? No.' Well, how can you feel it? It has been squeezed out. You are in such an awful state under the pressure of the body and the mind that it is very difficult for you to think rightly. Meditation, when it has developed, when it has become established within you, pushes this body away from your being. You feel as though the walls of the room have at last moved back and are now standing in the right position; you feel separate from the walls and not so pressed by them — just exactly like that, you feel the body has moved away.

That is not the last word, of course, but there comes a definite experience like this. And such a state is always accompanied by a change in the mind; I cannot have an ordinary mind and at the same time feel the body has gone from me and is not really imposing itself upon me. Our thought determines what the body does to us — and by the same token, what the outside world does to us. Only when your

mind has become free from the domination of the
sense world — of which the body and the outside
world are important elements — will you begin to feel
that the body has released you; you have become
free from its domination.

I remember long ago I read a novel by Victor
Hugo in which a man who, because he stole a loaf
of bread, was imprisoned for many years, and after
he came out he was like a brute. Then through the
influence of a Catholic bishop, he became a changed
man. Many years later, some bandits got hold of him
and in order to make him confess something put
some irons in a brazier and threatened to burn his
body. And he said to them, 'Oh, you want to frighten
me?' Then he took one of those red-hot irons and put
it on his flesh without flinching in the slightest. That
is a true-to-life story. You see, this man, under the
influence of the bishop, had become so transformed
that he had become exceedingly unselfish; he never
sought anything for himself. And because of his own
suffering in the prison and afterwards, he felt that he
should try to help others; he had no desire for his
own happiness. His self was gone to a great extent; so
what difference did it make to him if somebody
burned his body? He would not cry out in horror or
in agony. Literally it happens so. If I do not want any
pleasures of this body, whatever may happen to it will
not make me restless. Anything may happen to the
body; I shall remain calm, because I am really
separate from it. When I want this body, want to

enjoy through it, I become mixed up with it. So you see, this change must necessarily take place in the mind: our mind should give up the things of this world.

Now, if you look at it from another point of view, where do you think this ultimate Reality is? Is it somewhere outside of you? There is nothing outside of you. Do you know that? Of course, if you have not thought about this fact or experienced it, you won't recognize it. There is nothing outside of you. Everything is in consciousness. If you say, 'Why, there is the San Francisco Bay, there are the mountains, here is the city; all those things are outside of me!' But where do you perceive them? You perceive them in your consciousness. What is perceiving? To perceive is to be conscious of, isn't it? When you say, 'I perceive this', you mean, 'I am conscious of it'. Can you think of any perception without consciousness? Of course, we have been fooling ourselves, stupid that we are, in trying to explain how we perceive the outside world, forgetting all the time that there is no such animal as the outside world. There is no such thing at all, except as a convention, a strong convention, which we cannot shake off. Actually, everything is in our consciousness. There is a wonderful philosophical poem by the great Shankara, in the very first verse of which he writes, *viśvam darpaṇa-dṛśyamāna-nagarītulyam nijāntargatam*[3] — this universe is within me. How? Just as we see a city reflected in a mirror within our own room and forget it is really a reflected image and think it is outside. Actually speaking, *nijāntargatam* — the universe is included within me, because it is really projected by my own consciousness. But you would not appreciate this idea or be able to test it, unless the sense that you are the body has gone from you.

Our consciousness is cluttered with all kinds of things all the time, because that is what we want. How can we have the reflection of Divine Reality in our consciousness? All these things cluttering our consciousness have to be wiped off. Then only will it become possible for Divine Reality, the highest Reality, to be reflected there. That is the thought at the back of progress in meditation. Whether you like it or not, there is no help for it.

You will find in every religion that whenever a person is instructed to practise meditation so that he can have higher and higher spiritual experience, it is always presupposed that he will give up his preoccupation with the 'outside'. There is a wonderful verse in one of the Upanishads in which it is said, *parāñci khāni vyatṛṇat svayambhus–tasmāt parāṇ paśyati nāntarātman* – 'The Lord has so created the senses that they always look outward and never look within; therefore they perceive the outside things but

3. Shankara, 'Hymn to Dakṣiṇāmūrti', 1.

not the Self within.' *Kaścid dhīraḥ pratyag-ātmānam aikṣad āvṛtta-cakṣur amṛtatvam icchan*[4] — 'But a steady-minded person, a wise person, perceives this inmost Self; desiring immortality, he turns his sight inward.' You see, we are all looking out; therefore, what is within we don't see. But if we want to see what is within ourselves, then our vision must be turned within. That is where people find the greatest difficulty.

However, when you have succeeded in turning your vision within, your mind becomes serene. And although this process is partly mechanical, in the sense that for a long time you practise certain things every day, really speaking, it is so subtle that it cannot be forced by any mechanical skill. It has to come to you; therefore some say that without the grace of God you cannot realize that state. Almost all religions have emphasized the grace of God. Almost — not all. Buddhism, for example, doesn't believe in God or any such thing. Buddhists are very commonsensical; they say, 'You practise like this, you will get this result.' But Buddha led his followers through hard ethical and moral disciplines in the beginning, and later they had to practise renunciation to attain to this state of contemplativeness.

I should tell you here that if you ever turn your mind inwards, you perceive such wonderful things that you would not like to look outwards at all. It is

---

[4] *Kaṭha Upaniṣad,* 2. 1. 1.

said that if anyone has caught a glimpse of what is within, he will never again seek anything in the outside. That's a fact. Even if, because of your previous habits, you are inclined to look outwards, you find all the joy has gone from these outside things. You go through the habit of looking out and becoming restless, but there is no joy, no glamour left in the outside world, nothing left. And very soon you come back to your inner quest, and you make further and further effort. Once you have caught a glimpse of what is within, it will never be destroyed. You make more and more progress. Whether you do it uninterruptedly or interruptedly doesn't matter. Sometimes, if you have bad tendencies, they will force you back to old habits, but you will find them so painful that very soon you will make another effort to go within, until all obstructions have been removed. Most wonderful reality! What would you find outside? There is nothing here — nothing!

And one thing you must not forget: all that you see here is the effect; the cause is always more potent than the effect; the cause is hidden, subtle, it is not in the outside. We run after all these external things; they exist for one moment — the next moment they are gone. We can never hold on to them. But the causal thing, that from which all these have come — that is permanent. If we can persuade ourselves that this hidden thing is the real thing, then meditation becomes easier for us. The moment you sit in meditation, your mind will at once become serene. A friend of mine told me that in one period of his life, whenever he would sit in meditation, in one or two minutes he would become completely absorbed. It was like a force; it would just take him within. Well, these things happen when you have progressed in meditation.

Now, as I said, you become free of the body; mind becomes serene. Outside, all kind of disturbances take place—people are talking, there are other noises—you will not be aware of those things; there are sensations in your body, many thoughts rise in your mind—those things don't disturb you any more. Whatever you are meditating upon becomes luminous, joyous, and infinitely peaceful. Then when you come out of your meditation it seems to you as if you had been deep, deep down in a profound reality, a most wonderful reality, and the joy of it and peace of it suffuses your whole being; your face becomes luminous, serene, and looking at you, people marvel. That is when meditation has become pronounced. It is not by any means the highest state of meditation.

2

I think it might be helpful if I tell you here some of the essential things about meditation. You see, it cannot be had without concentration. Concentration means bringing the whole mind to one point and holding it there. That point is the object of meditation. Some people practise concentration in a mechanical sort of way; that is, they try to hold their attention on any object. If you are practising *rāja yoga*, the 'royal yoga', that kind of practice is very good. Of course, these practices, and, for that matter, any other spiritual practice, should be undertaken only with the guidance of an expert.

Now, let us speak of ordinary meditation. Here you will find that the object of meditation is oftentimes God Himself. There is a reason for this: the object of meditation should be something that can draw the whole of your mind. For example, you do not bring elementary problems to a great scholar; they cannot draw his attention. But if you give him a very profound problem then it will absorb his whole mind. In the same way, the object of your meditation should be such that in order to comprehend it you have to give more and more of your attention to it, until your whole mind becomes absorbed; otherwise you will not have proper concentration. Therefore, generally speaking, God is the object of meditation. God is one word, but God has many aspects, and you have to know which aspect of God you should meditate upon; it should have an affinity with your own inner being. Just as we have our likes and dislikes in everyday things, we also have likes and dislikes in spiritual things: you are drawn naturally to some aspects of God; other aspects leave you cold. But the object of your meditation should not necessarily be what you like *now*. You know how our likes change. I may like something today, but how am

I to know that I shall like it twelve years from now? So I have to have something by meditating on which —even though I may not like it now—I shall find more and more of my mind becoming absorbed in it. That is why, here also, you need the help of an expert.

Now, that's a very peculiar kind of thinking—that which is called meditation. Concentration means that your mind should not go to other things; it should dwell upon one object. But meditation is not thinking in an intellectual sense, or rather I should say it is not thinking only with the brain, as we are accustomed; it is thinking with our whole being. Say, late at night you are seated outside; nature has quieted down, and you sit there and feel that stillness with your whole being—that is not an intellectual experience at all, not a mere knowing with your brain. You just soak in the peace, and you feel better for it. Or when you are seeing beautiful scenery or hearing beautiful music, you will find that such perception is not intellectual; it is something deeper. Shall I say it is feeling? I should say it is more than feeling. Feeling, in the ordinary use of the word, is sometimes rather vague, but if I say it is thinking, then it seems to be a kind of dry process. Actually, it is a combination of both: there is knowledge and there is also deep satisfaction. I am inclined to think that all the different functions of our mind exist separately only in our present state, because we are disintegrated. But when we reach the state of unification, which is our true nature, then we find they have become joined together; and sometimes that state is called intuition. Well, in meditation you feel the object of meditation with your whole being, absorb it with your whole being; it is that process on which you depend.

How do you achieve it? There is really no royal road to it. They say that if you have a yearning for God, because of which you are meditating upon Him, then this state of mind will awaken. Or to put it in a different way, consider that the mind has two aspects—lower mind and higher mind. The lower mind is that part of the mind with which we are acquainted now, with which we think and plan all kinds of things. Then there is another mind above this which is serene and calm; serenity is its nature, and wonderful things are in it. It is that mind which is able to meditate in the way I have said. They say that when you struggle to concentrate your mind on the object of meditation—that is to say, when you try to perceive it clearly and at the same time try to have the right feeling about it, try to feel that this is the Lord, this is God—then as a result of that struggle, your higher mind becomes activated, wakes up, as it were. You suddenly have a feeling that you have experienced a reality you had never experienced before; it has nothing to do with this accustomed reality; it is infinitely superior to it. It is more interior than exterior; yet it is not a subjective condition. When once or twice you have that feeling, your effort at meditation becomes doubled. You feel a desire to capture that experience. Maybe for several months nothing happens, then you have it again, and you feel encouraged, and then when you try more and more, that experience becomes more frequent, until every time you sit in meditation your mind at once goes into that state; you feel that higher reality, and your effort is to go deeper and deeper into it, to have a clearer and clearer perception of it.

Of course, you cannot make progress unless you have practised a lot of self-discipline. Remember the verse from the Upanishads that I quoted to you — 'The senses are so made by the Lord that they all look outward and do not look within. But a wise person, in order to attain to immortality, turns his eyes inward and thereby perceives this inmost Self' — well, you must have that discipline; you must not let your senses run wild. When I see people talking about religion, arguing about God, and when at the same time I see no self-discipline in them, I say this is a travesty of religion and nothing can come of it, except further confusion of the brain. You can erect a powerful building only on a strong foundation. Discipline is that foundation.

So many odd ideas have spread in America because you haven't a strong spiritual tradition here. Now, I know some of you will be annoyed at my saying that. You will say, 'Why! We have the Christian tradition, we have the Jewish tradition! These are very old religious traditions.' But I must say this, although you have inherited these traditions and show interest in religion — look at all the churches and synagogues and so on! —you have never thought of religion as a personal experience. You have always emphasized belief and faith, and there is always a contractual approach to God: if you do such and such, then God will give you something. It is so primitive an approach! Excuse me, but that is how it seems to us. In India we also have that phase of religion, but long ago we recognized that it is for those who do not want real religion, yet want something. It is all right for such people to play with these ideas, but if you want to be truly religious or spiritual, you have to have experience. Faith and belief have very little to do with it.

Discipline is the word. You have to learn to discipline yourself. Many of you think that if you become disciplined, you will lose your spontaneity, your creativity—as if to be instinctive is to be creative! Well, maybe so. But the things that are created out of an instinctive state of mind are most horrible. That is not true creativity: it is mediocrity, even less than that—it is insanity. Creativity is a very big thing. There is only one Creator and that is God, and unless you go very close to God, to say that you are creative is nonsense. Discipline is the thing. Why? To get rid of the bad habit of letting your energies run out. A person has a little spiritual experience; at once he becomes eager to talk about it. He will give twenty thousand lectures, and nowadays you have so many opportunities of talking. First of all, you could lecture to a congregation; then you could lecture on the radio, or if you have more money, you could lecture on television. Your energies are continually going out. That's a deadly thing. You *may not* give out anything unless you have reached a state where the more you give, the more you are replenished. When a man starts a business with a small capital, he cannot spend the profits; he can barely live; he has to sink the profits into his business. For years and years he will do that. Then finally he reaches a state where he can enjoy the fruits of his labour; his business will not suffer. In the same way, you reach a state in your spiritual growth when, even if you give a lot, there is a perennial spring of power and knowledge within you; it has opened up, and you never lack anything. Even then, you do not become extravagant about it, and rarely do you expend yourself by your own will. There is another will then, which prompts you about what you should and shouldn't do.

So you have to discipline everything. All the senses are eager to contact their objects: our eyes are hungry, our ears are hungry — every part is hungry. Every sense has to be disciplined. And if you say that would be just killing yourselves, I shall accept that view in regard to most people. But then, the serious religion of which I am speaking is not for those people. Theirs is a ritualistic religion, an essentially active religion, in which there is very little contemplation; they sing loudly, pray loudly, do some physical movements, which are called ritual. That is good for them.

There was a great prophet born in Bengal several centuries ago. He taught love of God, but he made a division between his followers. The vast majority he taught to sing the name of God — loud singing, dancing, many drums, many cymbals — a wild affair. He himself would go into the streets and start singing, and thousands — the whole city, really — would come out and sing and dance in ecstasy. Being an Incarnation of God, he had that power. He also taught this class of people to practise kindness to every person and to serve the holy. But there was a smaller group to whom he taught all the mysteries of divine love: how to meditate deeply; how to attain a state of ecstasy where the soul can realize God's love and become unified with Him in deep communion, become totally absorbed in His love. He himself used to pass through three stages. There would be an external state of consciousness in which he could sing the name of the Lord and tell people about God; then there would come a state of ecstasy in which he could not speak but would dance in the joy of God. And then came an internal state in which he would become absolutely calm. Well, these last two states are for the minority, and I am speaking, of course, of that group.

And for them there has to be discipline. Discipline is not only of the senses but also of our energies. If you have no control over your energies, how will your thought become powerful? Unless your thoughts and feelings have energy behind them, they are pale and unreal. So you have to have energy, and you have to apply it to the right feelings and the right thoughts; then those thoughts and feelings become powerful and can attain what you want to attain. In the long run you will find nothing avails unless it is powerful. Mere piety is not enough. Yes, I like a pious person. What is wrong with piety? People say, 'Oh, so-and-so is so pious!' as if it were a matter for reproach; probably they think piety is superficial. But put energy behind it, then to be pious is wonderful. Everything requires energy. If there is no energy behind what I say, then I am only adding more noise to this noisy world. But if there is energy behind my words, they will go through all kinds of barriers and reach the quick of your heart and become effective.

In meditation you need energy. Just as a diver who wants to go to the very bottom of the sea can't do so because he hasn't the energy to counteract the buoyancy of the water, in the same way our mind wants to go deep, but there is no energy behind our efforts; so we are frustrated, we are pushed back to the surface. How will you get this energy? There is no lack of energy in anyone; only it is flowing in wrong directions. People say they have no willpower. Of course they have willpower. Just see all the wrong habits of thought and action we have; such tremendous power is behind them that we cannot withstand them. That is where your power is going. If you could bring that power away from there and put it in the right place, then you would say, 'I am *exceedingly* powerful.'

Well, that is called discipline. You have to practise those things. Now, when I put it in this way, it seems like a rigid routine, dry and forbidding, and I think some of you will say, 'That's not for us! There must be some easier religion.' But when you live it, it can be different. I am telling you all these things in an hour or an hour and a half, but in living them you will probably spend all your life, and if you live them every day, there is nothing forbidding about them. As a matter of fact, the life of a person who meditates regularly should be a joyous life. On the other hand, I should not give you the impression that from the very beginning it is all just great fun. No. There is a period of struggle. Who doesn't have it? When boys and girls leave high school and go to college, they are frightened the first year. Even intelligent boys find college life too much for them at first; but within one year they become accustomed to it. Spiritual life also is like that: struggle is required, but there is a joy in that struggle. If you know the traditions of spiritual life, you won't be discouraged. The traditions are that spiritual practice is a slow process and that what you gain through your spiritual effort is infinitely valuable. Even if it takes a long time to attain anything, it is worth doing, because what you attain will always be with you, from eternity to eternity. Just imagine this!

So many things we gain and lose. A musician has

to practise hours and hours every day, and for how long do you think he remains a musician? After some years he finds his body has become feeble, his voice has become feeble; he cannot sing any more, he cannot play any more. All these things happen, and yet how many years of his life have been devoted to this effort, how many hours of practice every day! And compared with that, even the little spiritual effort that you make from day to day in the beginning is infinitely fruitful. Actually, in the beginning you can't practise hours and hours with impunity. Until your whole body has undergone a change and your mind has fallen in line, it is dangerous to concentrate and meditate too long; there will be too much of a revolt within you. But even a little effort will bring peace and knowledge and steadiness and strength and purity into your life, and you will *never* lose those things. For a time they may become submerged, if you make mistakes, but they will never die; it is just a question of time before they again come out.

When I think about it, as I often do, I am really amazed at the grace of the Lord—or if you don't believe in God, then at the nature of the Self: with such comparatively little effort we gain so much that is of eternal validity; we become all transformed! Not merely do *we* become transformed, other people coming in contact with us sense the existence of something they could never have dreamt of before. One person, if he is peaceful, can bring peace to thousands without saying a single word.

I remember when I was studying in Calcutta, I was standing one afternoon just outside the gate of the college, and across the street a middle-aged woman was walking along. What a face! Quite clearly she had been to the Ganges, which was about three miles distant at that point. It is the habit of many Hindus, to walk before dawn to the Ganges, bathe there, and meditate for hours and hours; and then at noon, or after noon, they return home. You can recognize them by their clothes. You see, the Ganges is often very muddy, and so after one or two immersions their clothes become muddy. Of course they wash them, but they still look muddy, and that is what they wear to and from the river. Well, there was this woman going home—straight, serene, all the peace of the world in her face. How often I remember that face! She didn't say anything to me. I just saw her as she was going along. There were many other people also, but what a person! If you could have the peace of God in your face, one sight of you will remain a bright memory in someone's life. Life is, on all accounts, a sorry affair—how many struggles, how many troubles come! What do you need to keep you strong under the pressure of circumstances? It is calmness and peace. If you have it yourself it is a great asset. If you do not have it, and you have seen another who has it, that memory will stand by you like a strong friend.

Just imagine this! You can gain that peace if you practise meditation methodically and regularly and if you do it rightly and without hurry. Yes, at the beginning there are many contrary things within us. Don't become unnerved by that. Slowly work on and you will find that all the wrong things have been rooted out or burned out; your mind has become calm and serene and joyful. You will find that whatever duties you have to do, whether you are in the world or outside it, you are able to do rightly. Why should not a person whose mind is calm and quiet, who has been somewhat purified of selfish desires and wickedness — why should he not do everything most wonderfully well?

If you ask, 'Will all these uglinesses of the mind really go?' — yes, they will go. But patience, my friend, patience and perseverance. God is not at our beck and call. Mind is a subtle thing; who knows its ways? You can know the ways of a piece of stone; it is not subtle, it is gross. Mind is subtle; its movements are beyond its own calculations. So unless we have perseverance, unless we have enthusiasm and confidence, then, of course, we shall give up in despair. But hold on! I have not seen any person fail who has been persevering.

The most sure of all lives is spiritual life. But perseverance you must have; the right motive you must have. You will be surprised how many motives there are, but if you are really seeking God, if you are really trying to attain this wonderful state, however ill-qualified you may have been in the beginning you will find you are becoming endowed with all the

254 MEDITATION, ECSTASY, AND ILLUMINATION

necessary qualifications. But hold on! Don't compare yourself with others, saying, 'I am superior to this one; I am inferior to that one.' That is for fools. Go your own way. If you cannot run, if you cannot walk speedily, go creeping along, but don't stay in one place. Every day do your best, and as sure as the sun will rise, you will find you have attained to success; there is no failure in spiritual life.

And you will find there is a lot of joy in it. After the period of struggle is over, there comes a wonderful time. I don't say that there won't be any more problems; from time to time your mind might act against you, but you have learned how to fight it. And, you know, after you have brought the mind under some control, there is joy in fighting it. Just as tamers of lions and tigers like to fight them, you like to give a fight to the mind: let it play its tricks, you are not frightened by it at all. You find yourself completely the master. You will say, 'The mind cannot reach me. Let it jump around a little if it wants to.' That's the sign of the strong person. You have to have strength, then confidence comes within you. Children of the Lord feel confident. And then the fun of spiritual life begins. Still, you have to be very alert, because enjoyment, even spiritual enjoyment, has a little danger latent in it: you are apt to become careless.

Now, suppose you have been going steadily on and have been making progress in meditation. What changes have come? As I have already indicated, you become free from body consciousness, and, para-doxically, you find your body improves. I do not want to say much about that, because many people think that's the be-all and end-all of spiritual life — good health, youthful appearance, magnetic personality — these foolish people talk about such things. But they do come: health improves, mind improves, whatever talent is there becomes manifest; all the good things flourish. There is a song: a disciple says to his teacher, 'My being was like a cremation ground, a bleak place, and now, my master, you have converted it into a beautiful garden, full of bloom and full of perfume.' Yes, life becomes transformed; many wonderful things come. Your mind becomes more subtle, and with this subtlety you feel that it has also expanded; the sense of limitation has fallen off. You sometimes find that time and space are, as it were, modes of your own mind, and you begin to sense something beyond time, something beyond space. When you have progressed further, contrary thoughts or tendencies that are still in your mind in subtle form rise to the surface from time to time, and you are able to destroy them by a slight inclination of will. It is as though a seed, which eventually could become a very big tree, has just sprouted, and with a slight pressure of your finger you destroy the sprout. Big, powerful thoughts you cannot destroy that way; they become your master. But in that state, because your mind has become very subtle, your perception has also become subtle, and you can see the fine movements of thoughts. You can see the beginning of all kinds of troubles that could arise, and you can destroy them. The moment you do that, you find your mind expands and becomes purer and more powerful. That's the psychological part of it.

Then there is a perceptual part. You become aware of the existence of the Divine Reality more and more keenly. Of course, that was your whole object all along—to find God. In meditation you become keenly aware of Him. Outside of meditation you also become aware of Him: more and more you seek to dwell on Him in various ways. You repeat His name, or you just brood on Him as existing everywhere. You don't have to be told what to do; you will instinctively do those things. Your mind will dwell on Him always. When you have progressed further, the time comes when you can really commune with God. Communion is a word used especially to indicate great depth of meditation; when the soul comes very close to God—that is called communion. Just as the San Francisco Bay flows out into the Pacific Ocean or the Pacific Ocean comes into the Bay, in the same way your soul has come very close to God and just pours itself into God; at other times God pours Himself into the soul.

A sort of intoxication comes upon you, as if you were drunk. Whenever there is a sense of unification, whenever everything has really become unified for you, there is that sense of intoxication. And when that state becomes intensified, when communion becomes deep, it takes the form of ecstasy — your face will become red, your eyes will become tearful, you will not be able to speak; outwardly, there is an expression of deep joy. What goes on within, who can say?

Then comes the state of illumination — the word we use is *samādhi*. If meditation is that state in which there is no diversified thought, then *samādhi* is meditation at its deepest and most intense, most real; even small and subtle interruptions are not there. The mind has become so serene, so fine that Spirit, which is very close to the mind, becomes clearly revealed, and the soul becomes lost in It. There is no movement, nothing there. It is then that whatever barriers still remain are destroyed; no darknesses are left there. Darkness is finitude. When there is no longer any sign of limitation, no longer any movement in the mind, that is the state of illumination. God is seen clearly without any kind of medium.

3

Vedantic philosophers have made a lot of little divisions in regard to that state. Some say there are two kinds of *samādhi*; others say there are many kinds, and they describe them, but those are details. Two kinds are generally spoken of. It is said that when you reach that depth of meditation where you feel your oneness with God, but still feel a little distinction — that is the lower kind of *samādhi*. Sri

Ramakrishna described it in this way: if you put a stick on the surface of water, it will appear to divide the water; actually speaking, the water is not divided. Similarly, in that state a little self-consciousness remains on the part of the individual soul; he has become one with God except for a slight semblance of distinction. What are the external signs of that *samādhi*? Of course, the person has no outward consciousness. You speak to him, he does not hear; you touch him, he does not feel. Even if you put a burning coal on his body he will not be aware of it. But because there has remained a little individuality, he still breathes — long breaths; there may be a heartbeat, but very slow, everything very slow.

When he goes still deeper, even his breath and heartbeat stop. His body becomes, medically speaking, completely dead — except that his face is luminous. That is the highest kind of *samādhi*. It is a curious thing that even after actual death the face of a highly spiritual person becomes very luminous; what makes the face so luminous after the soul has departed is a fascinating question, but it is a noticeable fact. Similarly, in this highest kind of *samādhi*, where there is no sign of life in the body, when everything is completely extinct, the face is very luminous. Then the person comes down and slowly begins to breathe again. At first there are one or two long irregular breaths. Then slowly regular breathing begins. His hands might tremble a little; signs of life begin to come; his body becomes, as it were, again conscious. Then he is able to talk a little, very indistinctly. Slowly, slowly he comes down.

These are outward signs I am speaking of. Inside, because of complete absorption in God, anything that was a bar to the highest knowledge has been removed. What is knowledge? To know does not constitute knowledge. To know presupposes that the thing we are knowing is outside of us. When the subject 'knows' an object, he does not *really* know it, because he is outside of it. His knowledge is very superficial; it is knowledge only by courtesy. True knowledge is complete identification between the knower and the object to be known. Complete identification! If I am to know you, I must become you; I must make myself one with your soul, so that what you feel in your heart, in your mind, becomes known to me. That is true knowledge. A mother knows her child that way; because she is so close to the child she can feel the child from within the child — at least partly. Love gives that intimate knowledge, if it is a deep and pure love. Any kind of intervening agency which obstructs even in the slightest the thing to be known has gone. That is called the highest illumination, because the knower and the known have become one.

That state cannot be spoken of. Whatever name you give it, it is nameless, indescribable. In his lecture at Harvard University on Vedanta, Swami Vivekananda was asked, 'Isn't it a state of self-hypnosis?' You think and think and think about

Brahman, or whatever you call it, and then you think you have become one with it. He said, 'No. I shall say it is self-dehypnotization; we are *now* hypnotized.' And he pointed out that when a person with all the usual human frailties, uncertainties, doubts, and ignorances enters into that state he comes out of it a transformed being. You see, you can describe that state only by its effects: when an ordinary person goes into it and becomes enlightened, would you not say there is something extraordinary in it?

We are all destined to reach that state. Remember that. Otherwise, why is it that we want to know and know and know? Why is it that we cannot be lulled by fairy stories? We have to know the truth. Of course, we want now to know the truth about the material universe, but soon you will find that knowing such truth does not advance your quest very far. Then you will say, 'I want to know the truth of that which is underlying everything that is.' That is the quest for God, and when that quest begins, it will never stop. If you have not yet begun that journey or have not reached very far in it, what is your life worth? You are born, you prance around for a few years, and then you die. Birds and beasts and insects are also going through the same routine. Isn't it true? Some of you may speak with ponderous learnedness; others may talk foolish things, but all we really do is dance around in uncertainty, and then we go. That which we cultivate and develop is mortal and perishable. I think and think, and my brain makes bulges in my skull; I am a learned man — a little stroke comes, I have become an idiot. All my learning, all my thought, all my arguments — all vanish into nothingness. What kind of achievement is that?

But, my friends, if you achieve this illumination of which I am speaking, it will remain untouched for you always. You may not be able to talk about it to others in a learned way, but within the light will remain undimmed. That's the beauty of it. It is not dependent on the body or on the mind; it is Spirit Itself, which we are; therefore once we have achieved it we have achieved the all. Even if everything within us that is mortal is destroyed, we shall remain untouched; our knowledge, our life will remain undimmed. That is the most wonderful thing about it.

The way to it is meditation. Meditation is bringing the mind away from all nonsensical things and dwelling on that which is the most important in the whole world — God. Whichever way you do it, you will gain. If you do it rightly, you progress quickly. But even if you don't know the way but dwell in devotion and earnestness on god, you will find your mind itself will guide you; your mind will tell you what to do. Earnestness is the key to the whole thing.